21世纪高职高专旅游类规划教材

酒店面试英语

主　编　张　媛
副主编　侯　蕊　李欢鸽
　　　　戴　铭　张丽娜

北京大学出版社
PEKING UNIVERSITY PRESS

内 容 简 介

本书以英语面试环节为核心，重点提高学生的英语应用能力，把行业知识和英语技能有机地结合，形成了完整有序的内容体系，并通过面试前、面试中、面试后的解读，系统地阐述了酒店面试所涉及的各个重要方面。

本书主题鲜明、内容丰富、实用性和操作性强，可作为酒店管理、旅游管理和涉外酒店专业的教材，同时也可作为酒店及相关行业从业人员求职应聘的参考用书。

图书在版编目 (CIP) 数据

酒店面试英语 / 张媛主编．—北京：北京大学出版社，2020.2
21世纪高职高专旅游类规划教材
ISBN 978-7-301-31159-2

Ⅰ．①酒…　Ⅱ．①张…　Ⅲ．①饭店—英语—口语—高等职业教育—教材　Ⅳ．①F719.3

中国版本图书馆CIP数据核字 (2020) 第 022647 号

书　　　名	酒店面试英语 JIUDIAN MIANSHI YINGYU
著作责任者	张　媛　主编
策划编辑	刘国明
责任编辑	李瑞芳
标准书号	ISBN 978-7-301-31159-2
出版发行	北京大学出版社
地　　　址	北京市海淀区成府路205号　100871
网　　　址	http://www.pup.cn　新浪微博：@北京大学出版社
电子邮箱	编辑部 pup6@pup.cn　总编室 zpup@pup.cn
电　　　话	邮购部 010-62752015　发行部 010-62750672　编辑部 010-62750667
印　刷　者	北京溢漾印刷有限公司
经　销　者	新华书店
	787毫米×1092毫米　16开本　10印张　234千字 2020年2月第1版　2024年7月第3次印刷
定　　　价	35.00元

未经许可，不得以任何方式复制或抄袭本书之部分或全部内容。
版权所有，侵权必究
举报电话：010-62752024　电子信箱：fd@pup.cn
图书如有印装质量问题，请与出版部联系，电话：010-62756370

前　言

本书是为有意从事酒店业工作的求职者精心编写的一本英语学习用书，全书内容翔实，涉及酒店面试的方方面面，目的是帮助学习者在求职前做足准备工作，提升面试英语口语交际能力和应答技巧。

本书的内容结构及编写特色如下：

章节说明——提供面试前后及面试过程中应注意的行为规范，便于学习者扬长避短。

常用格式——解析了面试英语涉及的相关应用文写作。

常用句型——根据不同文体，汇集了相关句型，提供丰富的写作素材。

常用模板——针对英国和美国不同的写作习惯，展示不同的写作风格，以及电子邮件格式下针对不同主题的写作。

职场解密——节选了部分人力资源专家撰写的专栏，有助于学习者对职业素养的具体要求有一个大致的了解。

必备词汇——收录了与本课主题相关的词汇，帮助学习者轻松地掌握相关表达用语。

迷你问答——设计了招聘面试中最常用到的基本问答，帮助学习者掌握最基本、最核心的酒店求职英语，通过反复练习，达到融会贯通的学习效果。

实战演习——用真实的面试英语情景对话将学习者带入求职面试现场之中，学习者通过实训获得相关的知识和技能，为将来应聘积累经验。

轻松一刻——汇集了一些英语笑话，为英语学习带来一份快乐。

本书适合酒店管理专业具有初、中级英语水平的学习者使用。

本书由张媛（郑州旅游职业学院）担任主编，侯蕊、李欢鸽、戴铭（郑州旅游职业学院）担任副主编。

具体分工如下：本书由张媛总体策划和总纂，负责 Lesson 1，2，3，16 的编写，李欢鸽负责 Lesson 4，5，6，7 的编写，戴铭负责 Lesson 8，9，10，11 的编写，侯蕊负责 Lesson 12，13，14，15 的编写。在编写过程中，万礼豪程教学团队提供了多方帮助和便利条件。

由于编者的能力所限，如有不足和遗漏之处，敬请谅解并批评指正。

编　者
2019 年 1 月

目 录

Part 1
Before an Interview 面试前 ——— 1

- Lesson 1　Preparations for an Interview 面试前的准备 /2
- Lesson 2　Cover Letter 求职信 /7
- Lesson 3　Resume/Curriculum Vitae 简历 /21

Part 2
In an Interview 面试中 ——— 39

- Lesson 4　Personal Information 个人信息 /40
- Lesson 5　Personalities 性格 /45
- Lesson 6　Hobbies and Interests 兴趣与爱好 /51
- Lesson 7　College Life 大学生活 /56
- Lesson 8　Working Experience 工作经验 /63
- Lesson 9　Strengths 求职优势 /68
- Lesson 10　Jobs and Positions 应聘职位 /72
- Lesson 11　Career Planning 职业生涯规划 /77
- Lesson 12　Hotels & Hospitality Industry 酒店和酒店业 /82
- Lesson 13　Working Attitude 工作态度 /87
- Lesson 14　Tough Questions 常见难题 /93
- Lesson 15　Asking Questions at Interview 向面试官提问 /98

Part 3
After an Interview 面试后 ——— 102

- Lesson 16　Thank-you Letter 感谢信 /103

Appendix 1　Hotel Groups 酒店集团 /112
Appendix 2　Skills and Abilities for Hotel 酒店业技能与能力 /132
Appendix 3　Duties of Different Positions in the Hotel 酒店的工作岗位及其职责 /137

Before an Interview

面试前

Part 1

Lesson 1　Preparations for an Interview
面试前的准备

章节说明

面试是求职者与面试官的互动，如果能在面试中与面试官顺利沟通，并能够将自己顺利地推销给对方，对方会认为你的沟通和表达能力可以在职场中得到发挥。参加英语面试时，除了要了解面试的一般常识，还要针对英语沟通的特点和中外文化差异做一些特别的准备。比如，对自己进行正确的评估，对酒店集团的信息进行搜集等。

Pre-interview Tips—Be PREPARED	面试前的建议——充分地准备
An internship is a great way to get your foot in the door of job hunting, as many companies prefer to hire from within. The willingness to work for little shows companies that you're serious about putting in the work, learning the skills, and getting ahead.	实习是帮助你步入职场的很好的方式，许多公司喜欢雇用具有实习经验的人。在实习期，不为索取的工作表明你工作认真投入，学习了必要的技能，并且积极上进。

续

Pre-interview Tips—Be PREPARED

Internships can lead to jobs. In today's economy, many companies are turning to internships as a cost-effective way to vet potential future employees. If you put in hard work, demonstrate your ability to solve problems, and keep your chin up, your value to the company might be too big for them to pass up on. In order to build your vocational qualifications and succeed in the job interview, you should make preparations as given below:

(1) Do some research via the Internet, books, alumni, friends and relatives

① Know your target hotel: origin, history, vision, culture, core values, brands, service and products, target consumption group, market situation and the competitive situation among the whole industry, honors and awards, social responsibility.

② Know your target position: major function, job responsibility, required qualifications, knowledge and skills.

③ Know yourself: career aspirations, motivation, strengths and aspects to improve.

④ Collect information of the interviewers: his/her names (writing and reading), position and subordinate departments.

(2) Establish a professional personal image via your grooming and appearance

① Hair: Be clean and tidy; avoid any strange/exaggerated hair style/color.

② Face: For gentlemen, please shave; for ladies, please have appropriate make-up. Smiling is important.

面试前的建议——充分地准备

实习可以帮助择业。如今，许多公司认为实习期是审视潜在员工的最有成效的方法。如果你努力工作，能够证明自己有解决问题的能力，那么就不要灰心，你的价值对于公司而言不可限量。为了提升你的职业能力，并能在面试中取得成功，你可以从以下几个方面来进行准备：

(1) 做好前期调研，可以通过网络、书籍、校友、朋友、亲戚了解

① 了解你的目标酒店：起源、历史、愿景、文化、核心价值观、品牌、服务与产品、目标客户群体、市场情况、行业竞争情况、荣誉与奖项、社会责任等。

② 了解你的目标职位：主要职能、工作责任、任职资质、知识与技能。

③ 了解你自己：职业抱负、求职动机、优势与不足。

④ 了解面试官：面试官的姓名（写法和读法）、职务、所属部门。

(2) 通过合适的妆容建立专业的个人形象

① 发型：确保你的头发干净整齐，避免任何怪异夸张的发型或发色。

② 面容：男士请一定要刮胡子；女士可以化淡妆。同时，保持微笑也很重要。

Pre-interview Tips—Be PREPARED	面试前的建议——充分地准备
③ Dress code: Business or business casual is preferred; casual attire and jeans are not appropriate; professional, simple accessories and jewelry are appropriate. **(3) Get well prepared before the interview, both physically and mentally** ① Be energetic—Sleep well the night before your interview. ② Be punctual—Make sure your transportation to the interview is reliable. ③ Be considerate—Bring your cover letter, resume, certificates, reference letters and any other materials you think will be requested or helpful. Present these upon request. ④ Be non-hurried—If possible, schedule the interview when it's convenient for the recruiter and on a day that is less busy for you. ⑤ Be polite—Remind yourself to be professional and courteous to everyone you meet in the company throughout the interview process. ⑥ Be mature—Tell yourself to be confident, yet humble; relaxed, yet organized; and last but not least, smart and honest.	③ 着装：首选正装或者休闲商务款；休闲装、运动服和牛仔就不合适了。建议选择专业简洁的配饰和珠宝。 **(3) 面试前做好身心准备** ① 精神要饱满：面试前请保证充足的睡眠。 ② 面试要准时：选择可靠的交通路线。 ③ 考虑要周全：带上你的求职信、简历、资质证书、推荐信和其他你觉得有用的材料，需要的时候能够及时提供。 ④ 时间要充裕：尽可能地将面试约在面试官方便而你自己也不是很忙的一天。 ⑤ 举止要礼貌：在面试过程中，你要记住专业且礼貌地对待每一个在公司遇到的人。 ⑥ 心态要成熟：告诉自己要自信而谦逊，放松而不失条理，聪敏而诚恳。

Checklist before Interview	面试前的检查清单
① Be aware of yourself. (esp. your advantages and disadvantages) ② Have a general knowledge of your target positions and the real demand of a hotel. ③ If you are capable to do the job, you should present the examples to demonstrate it. And you should think about how you will let the hotel know about your capabilities.	① 认清自己的优、缺点。 ② 事先尽可能了解清楚应聘职位的要求和酒店真正的招聘需求。 ③ 如果认为自己可以胜任所应聘的职位，应准备好能够证明的具体实例，并思考如何让对方了解你的能力。

Part 1 Before an Interview 面试前

续

Checklist before Interview	面试前的检查清单
④ Prepare several questions and answers written on your notebook and bring it with your. Of course, you don't have to necessarily recite them all, for the recitation couldn't express your enthusiasm and you will look unconfident. ⑤ If you would like to know the hotel better, including service, marketing, training schedule, working conditions etc., you could ask the interviewers properly face to face. ⑥ Imitate a reality show of job interview when you have prepared several questions. Besides that, you can present it in face of your family or friends.	④ 准备一些可能会被问到的问题，并准备好相应的答案。把问题和答案写在小纸条上，面试当天记得带在身上。当然，即使准备好了答案，也没有必要背下来，因为如果你在回答面试官时像在背书的话，就无法将你对工作的热忱传达出来，也会显得缺乏自信。 ⑤ 如果想在面试时进一步了解酒店的服务、市场情况、培训计划、工作条件等问题，面试时适当请教面试官。 ⑥ 如果已经准备了一些预设的问题和答案，不妨进行一下模拟面试。当然，除了自己一个人练习外，也可以在家人或朋友面前练习。

练习

What are your steps in the interview-preparing process?

Summary	小结
Please prepare the following items before the interview: • A resume • A recommendation letter • Hotel information collected in advance • Questions consulting the interviewers • Pen and paper	面试前，请准备好以下物品： • 一份简历 • 一封推荐信 • 事先搜集的酒店信息 • 需要请教面试官的问题 • 纸和笔

职场解密

Make a list of work-related skills you'd like to learn. Your employer will be interested in hearing about how you intend to become a better employee. Think about which skills will make you more competent in the position you're applying for. Find some books and upcoming activities that would significantly improve your abilities. In an interview, tell the employer what you're reading and learning, and that you'd like to continue doing so. Here is a list of some of the most important job skills, wanted by employers, that a job-seeker must have to be sure of landing a good job and just as importantly, keeping it.

- ✓ Logical thinking and information handling: Most businesses regard the ability to handle and organize information to produce effective solutions as one of the top skills they want. They value the ability to make sensible solutions regarding a spending proposal or an internal activity.
- ✓ Technological ability: Most job openings will require people who are IT or computer literate or know how to operate different machines and office equipment, whether it's a PC or multi-function copier and scanner. This doesn't mean that employers need people who are technology graduates—knowing the basic principles of using current technology is sufficient.
- ✓ Communicating effectively: Employers tend to value and hire people who are able to express their thoughts efficiently through verbal and written communication. People who land a good job easily are usually those who are adept in speaking and writing.
- ✓ Strong interpersonal skills: Because the working environment consists of various kinds of personalities and people with different backgrounds, it is essential to possess the skill of communicating and working with people from different walks of life.

Lesson 2　Cover Letter 求职信

章节说明

　　求职信是推荐信的一种，目的是要试着去推销自己。撰写求职信应注意礼貌，还应注意内容的可信度，尤其在强调自身经历和优点等信息的时候，更应把握尺度。信中应说明欲应聘职位的名称；简述自身的经历、特质（集中于品格、才智、成绩、工作能力、学习能力以及社会关系能力等）、职业目标；曾经接受的专业训练、高等教育或者相关的证书、认证等；与所应聘职位有关的专业技能；表示期待与对方见面。因此，求职信必须采用能吸引读者注意力的写作风格，才能引起对方的兴趣。

Format	常用格式

There should probably be four paragraphs: ①Reference to the advertisement; ②Educational and work background; ③Why I want the job; ④Enclosures.
 	
  Specifically speaking, a cover letter should mention:
✓ How I hear about the job;
✓ Qualifications;
	求职信可以写成四段：①提及广告；②教育和工作背景；③为什么我想要这份工作；④附件。
	
	  具体地讲，求职信应该提到：
	✓ 我是如何知道这个工作的；
	✓ 我的学历和资质；

Format	常用格式
✓ Experience; ✓ Why I want the job; ✓ CV and photo; ✓ Prepare for an interview. 　　(1) Introduction—Reason for writing 　　(2) Central section (details) 　　① Background information about yourself such as achievement and experiences. 　　② Reasons for applying and required response. 　　In the body of your covering letter, mention one or two advantages, from the employer's point of view, of hiring you. Be sure to avoid dragging or being pushy and to maintain a polite, neutral-to-formal tone. 　　(3) Conclusion (action or response)—Suggest what the reader should do 　　The final paragraph should offer to provide any other information or details the prospective employer might want. 　　(4) Close 　　The ending of the letter normally is only one line sentence simply, which should correspond to the content of the letter.	✓ 我的工作经验； ✓ 我为什么想得到这份工作； ✓ 简历和照片； ✓ 准备参加面试。 　　(1) 开始段：写信的原因 　　(2) 主体部分（细节） 　　① 自身的背景情况，例如：取得的成就和经历。 　　② 应聘的原因和按要求所做的回应。 　　站在你未来雇主的角度上，在求职信中提及一两点他雇用你的优势。确保避免拖沓或咄咄逼人，并且应该保持有礼貌、温和正式的语调。 　　(3) 结论（行动或回应）：建议读信人应该采取的措施 　　最后一段应该给你未来的雇主提供一些信息和细节。 　　(4) 结尾 　　通常信件的结尾只需要简单的一行字。它应与信件的内容相呼应。

Sentence Patterns	常用句型
Introduction ● I'm writing to apply for... ● I am writing in response to your advertisement in *China Daily* of May 8th... ● I am writing to enquire whether you have a suitable vacancy for me in your hotel. ● I am writing to express my interest in your recently advertised position for a waitress... ● I am writing this letter to recommend myself as a qualified candidate for the job of executive lounge you have advertised in...	**引言** ● 我来信应聘…… ● 我来信是想应聘5月8日登载在《中国日报》上的一则招聘广告…… ● 此次致函是询问贵酒店是否有适合我的职位空缺。 ● 我来信是想应聘酒店服务员一职…… ● 我来信是想应聘贵酒店登载在……上有关行政酒廊的工作，我向您推荐我是一位合格的候选人。

续

Sentence Patterns	常用句型
• I write this letter to submit my application for... • I write this letter to apply for the position that you have advertised in *China Youth* Thursday... • I saw you ad for a (job title) advertised in the brochure/on the website. • Your advertised position of GM[①] assistant interests me... • I would like to apply for the vacancy of... • I wish to apply for the post...advertised in... on... • I was interested to see your advertisement in... and wish to apply for this post. • I understand from Mr. ..., one of your HR staff, that there is an opening in your hotel for... • Ms. ... informs me that she will be leaving your hotel on. ... If her position has not been filled, I would like to be considered. **Experience** • I have (number) months/years of experience in (job area). • My qualifications include a high school diploma and two professional certificates. **Personalities and Qualities** • I am a very hardworking person. • My qualities include persistence and dedication. • I am an efficient, hard-working, trustworthy and very personable employee. • I used my best endeavors at all times to perform my work conscientiously. • In my opinion, I have the necessary character, dedication and approaches to be suitable for the position of... • I have an outgoing personality and I mix well.	• 我来信是想递交有关……的求职信。 • 我来信是想应聘贵公司周四登载在《中国青年报》上的一则招聘广告…… • 我看到了贵酒店刊登在宣传册/网站上的招聘广告。 • 贵酒店有关招聘总经理助理的职位，我很感兴趣…… • 我来信是想应聘……职位。 • 我想应聘……日在……的招聘广告上刊登的……一职。 • 我对贵酒店在……上刊登的招聘广告很感兴趣，希望能应聘这一职位。 • 从贵酒店人力资源部的一位员工……先生那里获悉，贵酒店的……一职现有空缺。 • 本人从……女士处获悉她将于……日离开贵酒店。如果她的职位尚为空缺，我想申请该职位。 介绍经历 • 我在（某工作领域）有（多少）月/年的经验。 • 我的资历包括一张高中毕业证书和两张专业证书。 描述个性及才能 • 我是一个非常勤奋的人。 • 我的特质包括毅力和奉献精神。 • 我是一位讲究效率、工作勤奋、值得信赖、非常受人欢迎的员工。 • 我在工作中始终尽职尽责。 • 本人认为，不论从性格气质，还是敬业精神及处事方法上看，我都很适合做……的工作。 • 我性格外向，与大家相处融洽。

---

① General Manager 总经理

续

Sentence Patterns	常用句型
• I make my full contribution to a team and am popular with my teachers and classmates. • I made a substantial contribution to the work of the Student Union and always performed my work in a businesslike and reliable manner. • I enjoy good health and am a good time-keeper. **Goals** • My career goal is to work for a large, multinational hotel. • My aim is to grow as a professional and develop my skills to their utmost. **Close** • I'd be very pleased to meet with you at your convenience. • I look forward to discussing this opportunity with you further. • I look forward to hearing from you and being given the opportunity of an interview. • I hope you will consider my application favorably. • I look forward to the opportunity of attending an interview when I can provide further details. • I have enclosed my resume that outlines in detail my qualifications and experience. • Should you grant me a personal interview, I would be most grateful. • Any favorable consideration of my application will be highly appreciated. • Thank you for considering my application and I am looking forward to meeting you. • If you need to know more about me, please contact me at... • I look forward to meeting you soon. • I would appreciate your prompt reply. • Please call me if you have any questions.	• 我具有团队合作和奉献精神，深受老师和同学们的欢迎。 • 我为学生会的工作做出了很大贡献，在工作中务实高效，稳妥可靠。 • 我身体健康，而且非常守时。 **谈论目标** • 我的职业目标是任职于一家大型跨国酒店集团。 • 我的目标是成为专业人士，并将我的技能发挥到极致。 **结语** • 我很乐意在您方便时和您见面。 • 我期待与您更进一步讨论这个机会。 • 期待收到您的回复，并得到一个面试的机会。 • 希望您能接受我的求职。 • 期待能有机会参加面试，向您介绍更详细的情况。 • 随信附上我的简历，里面详细介绍了我的资质和工作经验。 • 如您能给予我一次面试的机会，我将不胜感激。 • 我将特别感谢您对我的求职予以考虑。 • 感谢您能够考虑我的求职申请，期待与您的见面。 • 如果您还想了解我的其他信息，可以通过……联系我。 • 期待很快见到您。 • 如能尽快回复，不胜感激。 • 如有问题，欢迎致电。

Part 1 Before an Interview 面试前

Model 1　Application Letter (Br. E) 英式求职信

写信人地址置于信的右上角	26 Windsor Road Chingford CH4 6PY
	15 May, 2018
其他细节信息按照完全平头式从页面左边空白处写起	Mr. W. R. Moore Personnel Manager Leyland & Bailey Ltd. Nelson Works Clapton CH5 8HA①
	Dear Mr. Moore,
说明应聘职位及在何处看到的招聘广告	PRIVATE SECRETARY TO MANAGING DIRECTOR I was interested to see your advertisement in today's *Daily Telegraph* and would like to be considered for this post.
概括介绍目前的职位和工作职责	I have been Secretary to the General Manager at Hill Hi Tech Machinery for seven years. As well as various administrative duties, I am required to attend and take minutes at meetings and interviews, deal with callers and correspondence in my employer's absence, supervise junior staff and other duties. I will gladly explain more in an interview.
说明为何对招聘的职位感兴趣	The kind of work in which your company is engaged particularly interests me, and I would welcome the opportunity. It would afford to use my language abilities, which are not used in my present post.
随信附寄履历及推荐信的复印件	My curriculum vitae is enclosed with copies of previous testimonials.

---

① 英国的邮编与国内的纯6位数字标示方法略有不同，英国邮编称为postcode，为英文字母及数字混合编码。

续

Model 1　Application Letter (Br. E) 英式求职信

得体的结尾	I hope to hear from you soon and to be given the opportunity to meet you at an interview. Yours sincerely *Jean Gray* Jean Gray (Miss) Encs.

Model 2　Cover Letter (Am. E) 美式求职信

写信人地址置于信的左上角	Your Name Your Addresses Your Contact details (phone and E-mail) May 15, 2019
其他细节信息按照完全平头式从页面左边空白处写起	Ms. Elizabeth Du Associate Director of HR Dept. ABC Company 6005 Shennan Avenue Futian District, Shenzhen 518000 Dear Ms. Du,
说明应聘职位及附寄了简历	Your job posting for a receptionist caught my attention straight away as my skills and experience are a close match to your requirements for this position. I would appreciate careful consideration of my credentials as outlined below and within the enclosed resume.
概括介绍目前的职位和工作职责	I have almost two years' work experience as a receptionist in a large organization responsible for handling all calls and visitors in addition to providing extensive organizational and administrative support.

续

Model 2 Cover Letter (Am. E) 美式求职信

说明自己的性格特点	I am a self-directed and independent worker who has taken the initiative to learn as much as possible about the company I work for in order to become a valuable information resource.
说明自己的优势	Among my particular strengths are my organizational and planning skills. I have developed a number of processes to manage my many work tasks and make sure I meet the demands of a fast-paced work environment. I utilize technology to assist me wherever possible and have a good working knowledge of a number of computer applications including MS Office.
说明为何对招聘的职位感兴趣	My strong communication skills and an outgoing, energetic personality ensure first-rate customer service to both clients and colleagues. I thoroughly enjoy dealing with a wide variety of people and take pride in being a receptionist.
赞扬对方，请求面试机会	ABC Company enjoys an excellent reputation and I am confident that I would be an asset to your company. I would appreciate the opportunity to discuss my abilities in more depth and am available for an interview at your earliest convenience.
得体的结尾	Please contact me via phone or E-mail to arrange a convenient time for us to meet. Thank you for your time and consideration and I look forward to speaking with you soon. Faithfully, *Jane Jobseeker* Jane Jobseeker Enclosure

酒店面试英语

	Model 3　Application Letter (E-mail) 电子邮件求职信
打开收件箱的页面	✉ **Inbox**
信件的主题（Subject）以及附件（简历）的命名要符合"SMART①"原则	**Concierge position**
	From: Frank Zhang <1234567@qq.com>
	Date: Thursday, May 18, 2017 5:10 PM
	To: Ricky Li < ricky.li@hg.com >
	Cc: Grace Zhang <grace.zhang@hg.com>; Christine Hu <christine.hu@hg.com >
	File : 1 Attachment (Resume-Frank Zhang. docx)
较为正式的称呼	Dear Human Resources Director Mr Ricky Li,
句子简洁段落简短。	I'm writing to apply for the position of concierge that I saw advertised in the subscriber of your hotel, IHG on the WeChat. My qualifications include a certificate from the Zhengzhou Tourism College, where I received hotel attendant training for one year. I am a hardworking and outgoing person. My other qualities include professionalism and resourcefulness. My career goal is to gain employment with a major hotel such as IHG.
段落之间空一行	I'd be very pleased to meet with you at your convenience. I look forward to discussing the opportunity with you in the near future. Yours truly, Frank Zhang
标准的"署名"模块	Frank Zhang 张诚 Hotel Management Major 酒店管理专业 Zhengzhou Tourism College 郑州旅游职业学院 1234567@qq.com |Tel: 186xxxxxxx

---

① SMART: Specific（具体），Meaningful（有意义），Appropriate（恰当），Relevant（相关），Thoughtful（周到）

续

Model 3   Application Letter (E-mail) 电子邮件求职信

📝 Compose
To
Add Cc
Subject:
Attach files
Content

Model 4   Cover Letter (Letterhead Format) 信头式求职信

写信人地址置于信的中间，模仿信封的写法	**Martin Liu** 136××××××× Martinliu1996@163.com No. 188 Jinlong Rd., Zhengzhou Tourism College Zhengzhou 450000 May 15, 2016 Ms. Dorothy Chen HR Director ABC Hotel No. 9 Xueyuan Rd. Haidian District Beijing 100080
美式商务信函称呼后可以用冒号	Dear Ms. Chen:
说明应聘职位及自己的求学经历	For the past two years of my undergraduate experience, I have become increasingly interested in the world of hospitality. I was very excited when I came across your internship opportunity through ZTC's Career Service Center. Banquet (Event) is an area of FB that immediately caught my attention and is something I plan on pursuing as a career path.

Model 4 Cover Letter (Letterhead Format) 信头式求职信

概括介绍有意义的社会实践	Last fall, I became a member of the ZTC's Pastry Club. This has given me a great opportunity to learn more about FB and to build a basic understanding of event knowledge. This experience has led me to dig deeper into my own passion for hotel. It has been a suitable supplement to my own research and reading on the subject of entrepreneurship. Our current portfolio size is ¥×××× which has grown from the ¥×××× of the college's endowment that we started with. After visiting your
说明对贵酒店集团发展的关心	website, I found it interesting that last November you acquired Starwood. I am a private pilot and my cousin works for Starwood, Meridien, Xiamen. I agree that merge is an expanding sector of business and therefore firmly believe this acquisition was a profitable investment. As a motivated student who has a deep interest in hospitality, I would like the opportunity to learn from your knowledgeable team of advisors. I am disciplined, reliable,
说明自己的优势	and have a strong drive to challenge myself. I realize that success may not come immediately, but through hard work, persistency and teamwork, goals that once appeared as dreams can develop into realities. I have enclosed my resume, which will allow you to assess my academic fortes and further evaluate my candidacy. Please feel free to contact me through phone, e-mail or the above campus address. I am available for an interview at your convenience. Thank you for your time and the consideration of my application materials. Cordially, *Martin Liu* Martin Liu Enclosure

Model 5 Application for Post of Hotel Trainee
申请酒店实习的求职信

写信人在这封求职信中叙述了自己的教育背景与学习成绩，这种写法适用于缺乏工作经验的求职者。

Dear Sir,

I would like to apply for the post of Trainee in your renowned hotel after listening to your "Campus Presentation".

I obtained practical courses in FB, Room Service and Reception Section at Zhengzhou Tourism College. ZTC awarded me a National Scholarship, which resulted from my hard work and contribution during my college years. Besides my major study, last year I accepted a temporary post with KFC in order to improve my English and gain some practical experience in dealing with customers. This work come to an end last month.

My special interest for many years has been hospitality industry and I should like to make it my career. I believe my qualifications in Hotel Management would enable me to do so successfully.

I am single and would be willing to undertake the internship away from home to Shanghai, where is a cosmopolis.

My former manager at KFC of Zhengzhou, Mr. Sun, has consented to act as my referee (telephone 0371-5×××8888), as has Mr. Li, Dean of Hotel Management, ZTC (telephone 0371-6113××××). I hope that you will take up these references and grant me the opportunity of an interview.

Respectfully yours,
Coco Li
Coco Li

Model 6 An Unsolicited Application 自荐求职信

自荐求职信是很难写的，因为没有广告或介绍人告知有关一份工作的任何情况。在这种情况下，你必须设法了解该公司的业务情况，然后在信中说明将如何用自己的资质和经验为公司效劳。

Dear Sir,

I believe that a large and well-known hotel such as yours might be able to use my services. For the past 2 years I have been a Hotel Management major at Zhengzhou Tourism College. I am now looking for a change of employment that would widen my experience and at the same time improve my prospects.

At ZTC I specialised in hospitality service and different posts' practice, and was awarded National Scholarship for my academic achievement and contribution. I thoroughly enjoy working at a hotel, particularly where the work involves dealing with customers.

Although I have had a little experience in customer research, I am familiar with the methods employed, and fully understand their importance in recording of buying habits and trends. I would love to use my services in your hotel of business type and hope you will invite me to attend an interview. I could then give you further information and bring testimonials.

I hope to hear from you soon.

Yours faithfully,
Samantha Ma
Samantha Ma

Summary 小结

As you proceed through your internship or job search, there are several guidelines that apply to each and every piece of correspondence you send out.
- Should be in business format.
- Should be on business stationery/resume paper.

随着实习和找工作的不断推进，你所寄出的每封求职信都应遵循以下规则：

- 应按照商业信函的格式撰写
- 注意使用行业要求的纸张

Part 1
Before an Interview 面试前

续

Summary	小结
• Must be typed (with the exception of hand-written thank-you notes). • Might become part of your permanent personnel file. • Know your strengths, abilities and career goals. • Take your time. • Always write to a person. • State the position for which you are applying. • Tailor each letter to the opportunity you are applying for. • Be brief. • Be professional. • Remember punctuation. • Indicate enclosure or resume. • Proofread, proofread and proofread.	• 必须使用打印的文档（除非需要手写的感谢信） • 可能是个人永久档案的一部分 • 了解自己的优势、能力和职业目标 • 不要慌张 • 注意读信人的称呼 • 说明自己应聘的职位 • 根据每次申请的职位对内容进行调整 • 语言简洁凝练 • 专业性 • 注意标点 • 注明附件/简历 • 反复校对

练习

Find a job advertisement in College Career Service Center and write an application letter. Include your reasons for applying and explain what you can bring to the job. You Should write at least 170 words but no more than 200 words.

职场解密

Cover Letter Checklist

✓ **Is your resume complete, including a review by a professional staff member?**
   YES   NO

You should never send a cover letter without a resume; therefore it is important to make sure you have finished your resume. Your resume and cover letter will be your introduction to prospective employers and require both time and attention before they are submitted.

✓ **Can you identify three or more unique features about the company and/or the job opportunity that you are applying for?   YES   NO**

It is important to know about the companies to which you are applying so you can accurately express your interest in them.

✓ **Can you identify your three greatest accomplishments?** YES   NO

It is necessary for you to know what your accomplishments and attributes are, so you can express them effectively.

✓ **Do they directly relate to the position you are applying for?** YES   NO

To effectively sell yourself as a candidate, you must be able to articulate what you have done that is related to this opportunity. Also, the prospective employer is looking for people who understand their industry and have related experiences or transferable skills to bring to the table. If you are not able to convey your abilities and talents to the employer, then she/he will not see your potential as a future employee.

✓ **Is there a specific position to apply for?** YES   NO

If you do not know what you are applying for, do not expect the employer to know if she/he should hire you.

✓ **Do you have a specific contact person to address the letter to?** YES   NO

A successful cover letter is always sent to a specific individual in the company. Letters with no name have a direct route to the recycle pile. Also be sure you have the correct spelling of the person's full name, his or her title, and the gender appropriate greeting (Mr. or Ms.). If you are uncertain, check this out. Call the company and ask for clarification or use the internet to review their website or latest annual report.

If you answered YES to all of these questions, then you are ready to begin writing your cover letter/letter of application. You have done your homework and it is time for you to start marketing your abilities to that prospective employer.

If you answered NO to any of these questions, then finish your homework! Any piece of missing information will only hurt your search and weaken the correspondence that you send. Your teacher will be happy to help you complete this checklist.

Lesson 3 Resume/Curriculum Vitae
简历

章节说明

"简历"简称 CV（美式英语称为 resume），英文的定义是"a short written document that lists your education and previous jobs, which you send to employers when you are looking for a job"。求职前，求职者应准备好一份整洁、及时更新的简历。简历完成后，请仔细检查全篇内容，不要出现错别字或单词拼写错误。简历应具备简明扼要、重点突出、排版精良的特点，最好将其浓缩至一到两页，方便招聘人员浏览和挑选。简历中须提及的信息有详细的个人信息、教育背景、资历和工作经验、劳动技能及兴趣等。

Keywords	关键词
● **Contact Information** 　　Name 　　Address 　　Telephone 　　Cell Phone 　　E-mail ● **Optional Personal Information** 　　Date of Birth	● 联系人信息 　　姓名 　　地址 　　电话号码 　　手机号码 　　电子邮箱地址 ● 可选性个人信息 　　出生日期

Keywords	关键词
Place of Birth	出生地
Citizenship	户籍
Visa Status	护照
Gender	性别
Marital Status	婚姻状况
Spouse's Name	配偶姓名
Children	子女
• **Summary/Objective**	• 求职意向
• **Employment/ Working Experience**	• 工作经历
Chronological Order	时间顺序
Positions	职位
Fieldwork	实地工作
Achievements	成绩
Responsibilities	职责
Job Description	岗位描述
Requirement	工作要求
• **Education**	• 教育背景
High School	高中
College (Dates, Majors, Degrees / Undergraduate)	学院（日期、专业、学位/在校生）
Pre-vocational Training	岗前培训
• **Professional Qualifications**	• 职业资质
Certifications and Accreditations	证书
Professional Licenses and Certifications	职业资格证
Memberships	会员资格
• **Skills**	• 技能
Computer Skills	计算机技能
Language Ability	语言能力
Technical Skills	专业技术能力
• **Awards and Honors**	• 奖励与荣誉
Scholarships	奖学金
Grants, Fellowships and Assistantships	助学金
• **Activities**	• 活动
Publications	发表刊物
Presentations and Lectures	演讲及讲座
Exhibitions	展览
Volunteering	志愿者活动
• **Hobbies and Interests**	• 兴趣爱好
• **Biography**	• 个人简介

Format	常用格式
The different types of resumes include **chronological, functional, combination**, or **targeted resumes** that match your skills to each job for which you apply: ✓ Chronological Resumes (most frequently used) ✓ Functional Resumes (focused on skills) ✓ Combination Resumes (skills and work history) ✓ Resume Examples Listed by Style Keep in mind that the format of your resume will vary depending on which type of resume you select. Use the following formatting guidance to generate a list of information to include on your resume, and then compile the details to format the information into a customized resume to send to employers. ● **Personal Information** In addition to your name, phone (cell/home), E-mail address, date of birth, city of residence (city, province, zip), and marital status. Your resume should attach a professional photo of yourself and state your language fluency. ● **Work Experience** Briefly describe your relevant work experience, listing the companies you worked for, the positions you held, dates of employment, and a bulleted list of responsibilities and achievements to attract the recruiter. For example, how you helped the company increase sales; how you solved specific problems; and volunteer activities you participated.	简历的格式包括**时序型**、**功能型**、**组合型**、**目标型**，结合每一份工作对技能的不同要求可以选用不同的模板： ✓ 时序型简历（使用频率最高） ✓ 功能型简历（注重技能） ✓ 组合型简历（技能和工作经历并重） ✓ 其他风格的简历 谨牢记简历的格式取决于你的个人喜好。根据以下简历模板的指导，搜集你想写入简历的信息，从而为自己定制一份简历。 ● 个人信息 个人信息除了你的姓名、电话、电子邮箱地址、出生年月、现居住地址（省份、城市、邮编）和婚姻状况，还应该附上一张职业照片以及说明语言的流利程度。 ● 工作经验 简单扼要地介绍之前相关的工作经验，包括之前就职的单位名称、岗位名称、工作起止时间。用项目符号有条理地罗列你的工作职责和成就来吸引招聘人员的兴趣。例如：你如何为公司增加销售额；如何解决具体问题；你参加的志愿活动。

Format	常用格式
• Education Like work experience, education is often described in reverse chronological order. After citing the dates, list the schools you attended, the degrees (major) you attained, any special awards and honors you earned and relevant certificates and training you received or are working toward. • Other Sections Depending on your experience and interests, you may wish to add other sections. E.g. objective, career summary/highlights and skills (computer skills or language skills) are optional. • References Common practice is to state "References available upon (on) request." Letters of recommendation may be attached to your resume.	• 教育背景 与工作经验一样，接受教育的时间也是按照倒序编辑。在提及日期之后，说明你的学校、所获得的学位、专业、奖项和荣誉、相关证书和培训。 • 其他部分 根据你的经历和兴趣，你可能想加上其他方面。例如，可以添加求职意向、职业规划、亮点技能（计算机技能或语言技能）等。 • 证明人 通常的写法是"如您需要可以提供证明人"。推荐信可以随附简历。

Model 1　CV (Br. E) 英式简历

		CURRICULUM VITAE
个人信息要放在简历的开头	NAME ADDRESS	Josh Carson 26 Windsor Road Chingford Essex CH4 6PY
可以选择是否提供这些信息	TELEPHONE DATE OF BIRTH NATIONALITY MARITAL STATUS	020 8529 3456 26 May, 1989 British Single
说明参加过的全日制的教育课程	EDUCATION 2007 to 2010 2005 to 2007	 Bedford Secretarial College (Secretarial Course) Woodford High School

Part 1 Before an Interview 面试前

续

Model 1 CV (Br. E) 英式简历

现在从事的工作在先，然后按时间倒序排列	**WORKING EXPERIENCE**		
	April 2011 to present	Personal Secretary to General Manager	Hill Hi Tech Machinery Vicarege Road Leyton London EI0 5RG
	Sept 19-- to March 2011	Shorthand Typist	Bains, Hoyle & Co Solictors 60 Kingsway London WC2B 6AB

具体列出所取得的资质和证书

QUALIFICATIONS
8 GCE A Levels
7 GCE O Levels

Cambridge	International Diploma in Business Administration	2010
LCCIEB	Executive Secretary's Diploma	2008
LCCIEB	Shorthand-120 wpm	2007
RSA	140 wpm Shorthand	2007

介绍个人所获特殊奖项

SPECIAL AWARDS
RSA silver medal for shorthand 140 wpm
Governor's prize for first place in college examinations

兴趣、爱好

INTERESTS
Music; Language; Hockey; Golf; Swimming

要至少提供两位证明人，可以是前任雇主或老师

REFERENCES
1. Dr. R. G. Davies
   Principal
   Bedford Secretarial College
   Righton Road
   Bedford MH 2 2BS
2. Ms. W. Harris
   Partner
   Bains, Hoyle & Co
   60 Kingsway
   London WC2B 6AB
3. Mr. W. J. Godfrey OBE
   Managing Director
   Reliance Cables
   Leyton
   London E10 5RC

按照月/年的格式来标注日期

June 2019

Model 2　College Resume Template (Am. E)
美式大学生简历模板

	Resume
个人信息要放在简历的开头	**1. Contact Information** The first section of your resume should include information on how the employer can contact you. 　　**First Last Name** 　　Street Address (*Home or School*) 　　City, State, Zip 　　Phone 　　E-mail Address
说明参加过的全日制的教育课程	**2. Education** In the education section of your resume, list the college you attend or graduated from, the degrees you attained, and awards and honors you have earned. If you are still a college student, or are a recent graduate, you may also include your GPA①. 　　**College, Degree** 　　Awards, Honors
现在从事的工作在先，然后按时间倒序排列	**3. Experience** This section of your resume includes your work history. List the companies you worked for, dates of employment, the positions you held, and a bulleted list of responsibilities and achievements. If you have completed internships, it's fine to include them in the experience section of your resume. You can also list summer jobs. 　　**Company #1** 　　City, State 　　Dates Worked 　　**Job Title** 　　● Responsibilities / Achievements 　　● Responsibilities / Achievements 　　**Company #2** 　　City, State 　　Dates Worked

---

①　Grade Point Average 平均成绩。

Part 1 Before an Interview 面试前

续

Model 2　College Resume Template (Am. E)
美式大学生简历模板

缺乏工作经验的大学生具体列出所参加的活动和在团队中的职位、所做的贡献 介绍个人技能（计算机技能、语言技能等）	**Job Title** • Responsibilities / Achievements • Responsibilities / Achievements **4. Activities** Include athletics, clubs, organizations and other college activities. If you held a position on a team (such as team captain) or in a club (such as president), you can mention this as well. 　Club, Club Position, Years in Club 　Sports Team, Team Position, Years on Team **5. Skills** Include skills related to the position / career field that you are applying for. These might include computer skills, language skills, or another type of skill related to the position. If you have any certifications related to these skills, you can list these here too. 　Skill #1 (related certifications) 　Skill #2 (related certifications)

Model 3　Chronological Resume 时序型简历

时序型简历按照倒序的方式罗列工作经验（从最近从事的工作写起）。这种简历的特点就是强调不同的工作经验。 现在从事的工作在先，然后按时间倒序排列	**Resume** **Paul George** 6 Pine Street Arlington, VA 12333 555.555.5555 (home) 566.486.2222 (cell) phjones@vacapp.com **Experience** *Key Holder*, **Montblanc** April 2016—Present • Organize over one dozen promotional events before and during opening of boutique, contributing to success of opening week, which saw revenue exceed projections by 18%. • Place orders to restock merchandise and handle receiving of all products.

Model 3 Chronological Resume 时序型简历

- Manage payroll, scheduling, reports, E-mail, inventory, and maintain clientele book and records.
- Implemented and integrated new register functions.

Sales Associate, Head of Women's Wear, **Nordstrom Collectors and Couture Departments**

July 2011—April 2016

- Provided thoughtful, convenient service to customers, earning annual customer service award twice.
- Promoted to head sales associate of designer women's wear due to merchandising ability and leadership skills.
- Singlehandedly set up trunk shows and attended dozens of clinics for new incoming fashion lines.
- Communicated with tailors and seamstresses to ensure fittings customers were 100% satisfied with tailorings and fittings.
- Scheduled private shopping appointments with high-end customers.

Bartender, **Jigg's Corner**

February 2009—July 2011

- Provided customer service to over 400 customers daily in fast-paced bar atmosphere.
- Maintained and restocked inventory.
- Administrative responsibilities included processing hour and tip information for payroll and closing register.

Education

Bachelor of Arts, **Ramapo College**, Arlington, VA, 2010

Computer Skills

- Experience with QuickBooks, NetSuite and other inventory management software
- Experience with social media and internet research

Part 1 Before an Interview 面试前

Model 4 Functional Resume for Management
管理岗位功能型简历

功能型简历注重技能和经验的介绍，多用于职场新人、想改变职业、从业经验有所中断或有某种特殊要求的工作等

对工作意向的描述

传统简历注重时间段工作内容的介绍，而功能型简历注重工作体验的获得及技能的习得

Resume

Jonathan Welch
5678 Ferndale Drive
Canfield, TX 44920
Phone: 1235554567
E-mail: jwelch@E-mail.com

SUMMARY

I am looking to put my management experience to good use in an entry-level leadership position in a customer service setting. I have proven myself to be a strong leader and am hoping to gain employment with a company that will benefit from my experience and passion.

EDUCATION

Worthington University　　　　　　　　　　　　2004 to 2008
Degree: Business
Grade Point Average: 3.2

MANAGEMENT EXPERIENCE

Assistant Manager
Hamburger Haven, Canfield, Texas
June 2007 to August 2008

Served as assistant to the restaurant manager and acted as manager in his absence. Supervised employee shifts. Made employee schedules. Conducted employee reviews. Disciplined employees when needed. Handled purchasing and accounting functions for the restaurant. Made marketing decisions. Hired and trained new employees.

Team Leader
Cellular Network, Canfield, Texas
November 2010 to December 2012

29

续

Model 4 Functional Resume for Management
管理岗位功能型简历

强调员工潜在的能力（特殊技能）是关键	Worked as a senior sales representative for a cellular phone provider. Trained and coached new employees. Led sales strategy meetings. Consistently exceeded sales goals. Supervised store employees during periods of management absence. **CUSTOMER SERVICE EXPERIENCE** **Customer Service Representative** ABC Products, Canfield, Texas October 2008 to October 2010 Worked in a call center handling customer complaints. Learned to deal effectively with difficult situations. Offered feedback to management to help set best practices for the call center. **SPECIAL SKILLS** I have experience as a leader, both among my peers and with those who have less experience. My experience in a call center environment helped to educate me about the processes and situations that arise in that type of atmosphere. I have the confidence to be able to enter a tough conversation with an employee. I am excellent at seeing the big picture and figuring out what needs to be done to provide the best service to the customer. I have proven to be a great motivator and enjoy encouraging others to perform their job to the best of their abilities.

Model 5 Combination Resume 组合型简历

组合型简历既强调技能又注重工作经历，而这也是许多雇主关注的问题。	**Resume** **Adele A. Jones** 1525 Jackson Street, Oakland, CA 94603 555-555-5555 E-mail: abc@abc.com
求职意向	**Objective:** To obtain a position where I can maximize my multilayer of management skills, quality assurance, program development, training experience, customer service, and a successful track record in the Blood Banking care environment.

续

Model 5   Combination Resume 组合型简历

第一部分类似于功能型简历，介绍技能、成绩、资历等	**Summary of Qualifications:** Results-oriented, high-energy, hands-on professional, with a successful record of accomplishments in the blood banking, training and communication transmission industries. Experience in phlebotomy, blood banking industry, training, quality assurance, and customer service with focus on providing the recipient with the highest quality blood product. Fully compliant with FDA CGMP, Code of Federal Regulations, AABB accreditation and CA state laws. Major strengths include strong leadership, excellent communication skills, competency, strong team player, attention to detail, dutiful respect for compliance in all regulated environments, as well as supervisory skills including hiring, termination, scheduling, training, payroll and other administrative tasks. Thorough knowledge of current manufacturing practices, and a clear vision to accomplish the company goals. **Professional Accomplishments:** • Facilitated educational projects successfully over the past two years for Northern California blood centers, an FDA regulated manufacturing environment, as pertaining to CGMP, CFR's, CA state and American Association of Blood Bank (AABB) regulations, and assure compliance with 22 organization quality systems. • Provided daily operational review/quality control of education accountability as it relates to imposed government regulatory requirements in a medical environment. • Assisted other team members in vein-punctures, donor reaction care, and providing licensed staffing an extension in their duties by managing the blood services regulations documentation (BSD's) while assigned to the self-contained blood mobile unit (SCU). • Successfully supervised contract support for six AT&T Broadband systems located in the Bay Area. Provided customer intervention/resolution, training in telephony and customer care, manpower scheduling, quality control, payroll, and special projects/plant extensions and evaluations to ensure proper end-of-line and demarcation signal. • Reduced employee turnovers, introduced two-way communication to field employees, enhanced employee appearance, and spearheaded the implementation of employee (health) benefits.

Model 5　Combination Resume 组合型简历

第二部分描述工作经历的大致时间表。	• Supervised and maintained the position of System Technician in charge of status monitoring and the integration of monitoring devices in nodes and power supplies. For the reception and transmission of telemetry to the network operation centers (NOC's) located in Denver, CO and Fremont, CA. Designed plant extensions, improved the paper flow and inventory control for the warehouse. Provided preventative maintenance at the system level, face-to-face customer interaction when required, and traveled to several telephony/@home systems in the U.S. for evaluation and suggestions in using the status monitoring equipment. **Work History:** • Acting Education Manager, American Red Cross, Oakland, CA: 2016—present • Education Coordinator, American Red Cross, Oakland, CA: 2011—2015 • Phlebotomist, American Red Cross, Oakland, CA: 2008—2010 • Cable Television CATV Supervisor, Core Communication Inc, Sunnyvale, CA: 2004—2007 • CATV System Technician, TCI Cablevision Inc, Fremont, CA: 2000—2003 • Technician/Day Shift Supervisor, Avantek Inc, Milpitas, CA: 1996—1999 **Education:** • Associate of Art, Administration of Justice, San Jose University, San Jose, CA • NCTI Certified, CATV System Technician, Denver, CO. • ABM Certified, Cornerstone Technician, Denver, CO.

Model 6　Customized Resume 自制简历

Resume

Name: Lei Wei (Clark)
Date of Birth: Dec. 20, 1991　　**Major:** Hotel Management
Height: 176cm　　**Weight:** 70kg
Telephone number: 159××××××××
E-mail: 567890@qq.com

PHOTO

Part 1 Before an Interview 面试前

续

Model 6　Customized Resume 自制简历

Objective: Seeking a position as a front office staff

Education:
2012.09—2015.07　Zhengzhou Tourism College, Hotel Management
2010.09—2012.07　Xinyang High School, Liberal Arts

Curricula:
Hotel Management
Laws and Regulations in Hotel Industry
Hotel English
Secretary in Hotel Industry
Business Etiquette
Sales and Marketing in Hotel Industry

Awards:
2014—2015　Excellent leader of the college Student Council
2015—2016　National Inspiration Scholarship

Skills:
English: Fluent in listening, speaking, reading and writing
Computer: Familiar with office application softwares

Qualifications:
2016.04　Driver's License
2015.12　National Computer Certificate
2015.09　CET 4

Experience:
2015.07—2015.08　　　Front Office　　　Hangzhou Friendship Hotel

Self-evaluation:
I am proactive, adaptable and honest, familiar with hotel operation, especially with front desk. I am good at using computers and fluent in written and verbal English. I have some experiences in customer service and have better coordinative ability.

　　表格型的简历适合工作经验不多的大学生，对于个人荣获奖励、资格证书、技能等应予以适当的分类，按照重要程度和时间顺序来进行分层。
　　简历需要突出个性化，反映你的求职意向和能力，可以根据个人经历来选择能突出个人技能的模块。

Model 7　Format Resume 表格型简历

RESUME

NAME: ZHENG TING

PERSONAL INFORMATION	ENGLISH NAME	Rose	AGE	20
	GENDER	Female	NATIONALITY	Chinese
	DATE OF BIRTH	July15th, 1995	MAJOR	Hotel Management
	COLLEGE	Zhengzhou Tourism College	E-MAIL	133×××××××@163.com
	CELL PHONE NUMBER	+86 133××××××××	DATE OF GRADUATION	June 30th, 2017
ENDUCATION	2014—present: Studying in Zhengzhou Tourism College 2011—2014: Studied in Huangchuan High School			
WORK EXPERIENCE	09/2014: Worked as a volunteer in the college orientation activities 05/2014: Worked as a waitress in F&B Department of Yuda Palace Hotel, Zhengzhou 07/2013—08/2013: Worked as a waitress in a restaurant in Shanghai			
SPECIAL SKILLS	Computer: Frequent user of Microsoft Office Language: English as a working language in hospitality field Practices: Serving the dishes; laying the tables; making up rooms; making reservations for guests with opera system			
HONORS	◆ National Grants from 2014 to 2015 ◆ National Scholarship in 2015 ◆ Excellent Leader of the College Student Council in 2014			
MAJOR COURSES	◆ Hotel English ◆ Opera ◆ Operation and Management of Front Office ◆ College English			
PERSONALITY	Confident, responsible, cooperative and honest			

Part 1
Before an Interview 面试前

Summary	小结
CV Length: Resumes are one page long. **Font and Size:** Times New Roman, Arial, Calibri, or a similar font is best. Your font size should be between 10 and 12 points, although your name and the section headings can be a little larger and/or bolded. **Format:** However you decide to organize the sections of your CV, be sure to keep each section uniform. **Accuracy:** Be sure to edit your CV before sending it. Check spelling, grammar, tenses, names of companies and people, etc. Have a friend or career service counselor check over your CV as well. **Contact Information:** At the top of your CV, include your name and contact information (address, phone number, E-mail address, etc.). Outside of the US, many CVs include even more personal information, such as gender, date of birth, marital status, etc. **Education:** This may include college and graduate study. Include the school attended, dates of study, and degree/diploma received. **Awards and Honors:** This may include college's list standings, departmental awards, scholarships, fellowships, and membership in any honors associations. **Thesis/Dissertation:** Include your thesis or dissertation title. You may also include a brief sentence or two on your paper, and/or the name of your advisor. **Work Experience:** List relevant work experience; this may include non-academic work that you feel is worth including. List the employer, position and dates of employment. Include a brief list of your duties and/or accomplishments.	**简历的长度**：尽量1页 **字体和字号**：最好使用清晰的 Times New Roman, Arial, Calibri 字体。使用五号到小四号字号，姓名和开头部分可以使用稍大些的字号或是加粗。 **格式**：可以选择喜欢的模板设计，但要确保每部分格式统一。 **准确性**：发送前一定要校对，检查拼写、语法、时态、公司及人名等是否正确。也可以请朋友或职业咨询师来帮助检查。 **联系方式**：简历的开头要有联系方式，包括姓名、地址、电话、电邮地址等。美国以外的其他说英语的国家还喜欢添加个人信息，如性别、出生年月、婚姻状况等。 **教育背景**：包括大学及毕业学校，包括学校名称、学习时间和所获学位、学历等。 **奖励和荣誉**：包括院级优秀学生、系部奖励、奖学金、助学金、任何荣誉协会的成员等。 **毕业论文**：包括论文的题目，可对论文进行一两句的概括或提及导师姓名。 **工作经验**：罗列相关工作经验，还可以包括你觉得有价值的非学术型工作。提及雇主、岗位、任职时间。简要罗列工作职责和成绩。

续

Summary	小结
Skills: This may include language skills, computer skills, administrative skills, etc. **Extracurricular Activities:** Include any volunteer or service work you have done, as well as any clubs or organizations to which you have belonged. You can also include any overseas study stours or internship program here if you have not already mentioned them.	**技能**：包括语言技能、计算机技能、管理技能等。 **课余活动**：包括志愿者活动、服务型活动及你所参加的社团、俱乐部等；海外求学或是访学、实习项目的经历等。

练习

Based on the following CV sample, modify your own personal information and design a resume of yourself.

Allen (Yan Fang)

(86)133××××××××

allenyanfang@123.com

EDUCATION

Sept. 2015—Present, Shanghai University, BE
- Candidate for Bachelor in Mechanical Engineering (ME)
- Major academic courses: Company Property Management, Marketing, Technology Communication, Information Management System, Modern Fabrication System

May 2018, Certified Public Accounting Training (CPA)

EMPLOYMENT HISTORY

Dec. 2018—Present, ITT Flygt Investment, China

Application Engineer, Sales & Marketing
- Achieve sales budget goals through application support and new industry market application research.
- Pay visits to end users and DI for seminars and technical presentations with salespersons or distributors while collecting marketing information and competitor information analysis.

July 2018—Sept. 2018, Intel Products Co., Shanghai, China

CPU Assembly Engineer (Internship)
- Analyzed yield ratio trends, documented and solved current problems.

- Participated in and helped oversee the training of marketing, business process modeling, and analysis at Intel University.
- Developed and led a project review with multi-media animation, which was highly appreciated by department manager.

June 2017—July 2017, GF Fund Management Co., Ltd.
Campus Intern
- Analyzed investment principles and related financially derived products.
- Formulated the scheme of market popularization and network marketing.

AWARDS
- 2016—2017, Scholarship for Excellent Students of Shanghai University
- 2015—2016, Image Ambassador of Shanghai Tennis Popularization Prize

COMPETENCIES & INTERESTS

English Ability: Band 6; intermediate competency
German Ability: 600 hours of Germany lessons at Tongji University
Computer Skills:
- National Computer Level 3rd Certificate (Network Communication)
- Professional Certificate of Assistant Information Officer (AIO)
- Fluent in: C++, VBA, Provision, JMP, AutoCAD, 3Dsmax, Photoshop, Solidworks, Aftereffect

Personal Interests:
Basketball; Speed Skating; Snooker

职场解密

The Top 7 Skills Employers Want

What skills are most important for companies that are hiring? There are some skills and qualities that employers require of all applicants for employment, regardless of the position they are hiring for. These are called soft skills, and they include the interpersonal skills and attributes you need to succeed in the workplace. In addition, there are the more tangible skills you need in order to do the job effectively. These are called hard skills, and they are the specific knowledge and abilities required to do the job. Here's information on the difference between hard skills and soft skills. You'll need both for most jobs, and it's important to show employers that you have the skills they need when you're applying and interviewing for jobs.

Here are some of the skills that employers consider as most important when recruiting and hiring employees. In order to get your application noticed, be sure to incorporate the skills you have that are required for the position for which you are applying in your resume and cover letter.

Also highlight your most relevant skills during job interviews.

1. Analytical

Employees need to be able to figure things out, so you will need to have some analytic skills to succeed in the workplace. The skills you need and the level of skills required will vary depending on the job and the industry. In conjunction with being able to analyze, employees are expected to be able to organize, plan and prioritize effectively.

2. Communication

The ability to communicate effectively, both verbally and in writing, is essential, no matter what job you have or industry you work in. You will need to be able to communicate effectively with employees, managers, and customers in-person, online, in writing and/or on the phone.

3. Interpersonal

Interpersonal skills, also known as people skills, are the skills you use to interact and engage with people. I just heard about someone who was hired because of his ability to connect with people. That trumped the other skills the employer was seeking, so be sure yours are up to par. Your interpersonal skills will be evaluated during your job interviews, so it's important to prepare for the interview so you are as comfortable and confident as possible when interviewing.

4. Leadership

When companies hire for leadership roles they seek employees who can successfully interact with employees, colleagues, clients and others. Even if you're not applying for management jobs, leadership is a valuable skill to bring to the employer.

5. Positive Attitude

Attitude might not be everything, but it's extremely valuable. Employers want employees who are positive, even in stressful and challenging circumstances. They want to hire applicants with a "can do" attitude, who are flexible, dedicated and who are willing to contribute extra, if necessary, to get the job done.

6. Teamwork

Regardless of the job, employers want to hire people who are team players who are cooperative and work well with others. They don't want employees who are difficult to work with. When you are interviewing, be sure to share examples of how you worked well on a team.

7. Technical

The technical skills you need will vary, of course, depending on the job. However, most positions require at least some technical skills.

Part 2

In an Interview

面试中

Lesson 4 Personal Information
个人信息

章节说明

　　面试时，面试官一般要求求职者进行自我介绍，目的是对求职者有一个大概了解，进而判断求职者是否适合这个职位，是否适合在公司工作。

　　求职者在进行自我介绍时要尽量引起面试官的注意并给对方留下良好的印象，如果求职者的自我介绍让对方没有丝毫的兴趣，面试就很难有效地进行下去。个人信息的介绍要避免冗长，尽量用简练的文字将自己介绍给面试官。

典型问题

Tell me about yourself.
介绍一下你自己。

相似问题

1. Can you make a brief introduction about yourself?
能简要介绍一下你自己吗？

Part 2
In an Interview 面试中

2. How would you describe yourself?
你认为自己是个怎样的人？
3. Could you introduce yourself, please?
能介绍一下自己吗？

Words and Phrases	必备词汇
brief [bri:f] *adj.* 简短的，简洁的	nationality [ˌnæʃəˈnælɪtɪ] *n.* 国籍，民族
introduction [ˌɪntrəˈdʌkʃ(ə)n] *n.* 介绍	telephone number 电话号码
describe [dɪˈskraɪb] *vt.* 描述，形容；描绘	E-mail 电子邮箱
introduce [ɪntrəˈdjuːs] *vt.* 介绍；引进；提出	graduate [ˈgrædʒʊəɪt] from 毕业于
outgoing [ˈaʊtgəʊɪŋ] *adj.* 对人友好的，开朗的	ID card 身份证
easygoing [ˈiːziˌgəʊɪŋ] *adj.* 轻松的；脾气随和的	comfortable [ˈkʌmftəbl] *adj.* 舒适的，舒服的
communicate [kəˈmjuːnɪkeɪt] with 交流	internship [ˈɪntɜːnʃɪp] *n.* 实习期
intern [ˈɪntɜːn] *n.* 实习生	interview [ˈɪntəvjuː] *vt.&n.* 面试
global [ˈgləʊb(ə)l] *adj.* 全球的	interviewer [ˈɪntəvjuːə(r)] *n.* 面试官
opportunity [ɒpəˈtjuːnɪtɪ] *n.* 时机，机会	interviewee [ˌɪntəvjuːˈiː] *n.* 被面试的人
improve [ɪmˈpruːv] *vt.* 改善，增进；提高	applicant [ˈæplɪkənt] *n.* 求职人，应聘者
current address [əˈdres] 目前住址	English name 英文名
city [ˈsɪtɪ] *n.* 市	family name 姓
district [ˈdɪstrɪkt] *n.* 区	given name 名
province [ˈprɒvɪns] *n.* 省	full name 全名
age [eɪdʒ] *n.* 年龄	gender [ˈdʒendə] *n.* 性别
birth date 出生日期	female [ˈfiːmeɪl] *adj.* 女性
birthday [ˈbɜːθdeɪ] *n.* 生日	male [meɪl] *n.* 男性
height [haɪt] *n.* 身高	native place 籍贯
cm=centimeter [ˈsentɪmiːtə(r)] *n.* 厘米	birthplace [ˈbɜːθpleɪs] *n.* 出生地
weight [weɪt] *n.* 体重	county [ˈkaʊntɪ] *n.* 郡，县
kg=kilogram [ˈkɪləʊgræm] *n.* 公斤，千克	house number 门牌
health [helθ] *n.* 健康状况	certificate [səˈtɪfɪkɪt] *n.* 证书
hometown [ˈhəʊmˈtaʊn] *n.* 家乡	CET 4/6 = College English Test Band 4/6 大学英语四/六级考试

Mini Dialogues	迷你问答
Q: Name and number, please? A: My name is Su Linlin. I'm Number 16. Q: Tell me a little bit about yourself, please. A: My name is Su Linlin, and I live in Zhengzhou. I was born in 1995. I am a student of Zhengzhou Tourism College, majoring in Hotel Management. I will graduate next June. I am an outgoing and easygoing girl and always happy to communicate with others. Besides, I like traveling very much and enjoy music. I'd like to work for your hotel as an intern. As a global hotel, I believe your hotel will provide me a lot of opportunities to improve myself. Thank you. Q: When were you born? A: I was born on April 10th, 1994. Q: What is your current address? A: No. 1 Yuying Road, Guancheng District, Zhengzhou. Q: Where are you from? A: I am from Luoyang, Henan Province. Q: May I know your age? A: Yes, I am 21 years old. Q: What is your nationality? A: The Hui nationality. Q: What is your telephone number? A: My telephone number is 13800138000. Q: What's your E-mail address? A: My E-mail address is sulinlin100@163.com. Q: When will you graduate? A: I will graduate in June, 2017.	Q：请问您的名字和面试号码？ A：我叫苏琳琳，是第16号。 Q：请简要介绍一下自己。 A：我叫苏琳琳，郑州人，生于1995年。我是郑州旅游职业学院酒店管理专业的一名在校生，明年6月毕业。我性格外向，脾气随和，非常喜欢与人交流。另外，我喜欢旅游和音乐。我想应聘贵酒店的实习生岗位。作为一家国际性酒店，相信在这里我一定能获取很多提升自己的机会。谢谢。 Q：你什么时候出生的？ A：1994年4月10日。 Q：现在住哪里？ A：郑州市管城区豫英路1号。 Q：你是哪里人？ A：我是河南洛阳人。 Q：能告我你的年龄吗？ A：可以，我21岁。 Q：你是什么民族？ A：回族。 Q：你的电话号码是多少？ A：我的电话号码是13800138000。 Q：你的邮件地址是什么？ A：我的邮件地址是sulinlin100@163.com。 Q：你什么时间毕业？ A：我将于2017年6月毕业。

Part 2

In an Interview 面试中

Situational Dialogue 1

A: Would you like to make a brief introduction about yourself?

B: Sure. My name is Su Linlin. I come from Henan. I'm 21 years old.

A: Where do you live now?

B: I live in Zhengzhou. The address is No. 1 Yuying Road, Guancheng District.

A: Have you got married?

B: Not yet.

A: Can I have a look at your ID Card?

B: Certainly. Here you are.

A: Thank you.

实战演习 1

A：您能做一个简要的自我介绍吗？

B：当然。我叫苏琳琳，来自河南。今年21岁。

A：您现在住在哪里？

B：我住郑州。地址是管城区豫英路1号。

A：你结婚了吗？

B：还没有。

A：我可以看一下你的身份证吗？

B：当然可以，给你。

A：谢谢。

Situational Dialogue 2

A: Come in, please.

B: Good morning, sir!

A: Good morning, please make yourself comfortable.

B: Thank you, sir.

A: Your name and number, please?

B: My name is Qiao Zhitao, number 10.

A: Pardon?

B: Qiao Zhitao. Q-I-A-O for Qiao and Z-H-I-T-A-O for Zhitao.

A: Yes, Mr Qiao, when were you born?

B: I was born on July 16th, 1995. I'm 21 years old.

A: Where do you live?

B: I am living in No. 15 Xizang Road.

A: Where do you come from?

B: I am from Kaifeng, a very famous city in Henan province with a long history.

A: Why would you come to Shanghai for your internship?

B: I love this big and modern city. I want to work in Shanghai.

实战演习 2

A：请进。

B：早上好，先生。

A：早上好，请随意。

B：谢谢。

A：您的名字及面试号码是多少？

B：我叫乔志涛，面试号码是10号。

A：请再讲一遍。

B：乔志涛。Q-I-A-O，乔。Z-H-I-T-A-O，志涛。

A：好，乔先生。您的出生年月是？

B：我生于1995年，7月16日。今年21岁了。

A：您住在哪里？

B：西藏路15号。

A：您家乡是哪儿？

B：我来自开封，河南省的一个历史名城。

A：你为什么要来上海实习？

B：我喜欢这个时尚大都市，而且想在这儿工作。

43

Situational Dialogue 2	实战演习 2
A: Can you leave your phone number and your E-mail address? B: Of course. My phone number is 18618610010 and E-mail is qiaozhitao95@126.com.	A：您能留下电话和邮箱吗？ B：当然。我的电话号码18618610010，邮箱地址是 qiaozhitao95@126.com。

练习

Tell me a little bit about yourself, please.
（name, age, hometown, college, graduation time, hobbies and so on）

....
....
....
....
....

轻松一刻

A Joke

Tom: (putting down two pence) A piece of bread, please.

Baker: It's two and a half pence now. Bread's risen in price.

Tom: When?

Baker: This morning.

Tom: All right, madam. Give me one of yesterday's.

Lesson 5　Personalities 性格

章节说明

　　不同的工作岗位对在岗人员的性格要求不同，求职者在面试时需要注意结合自身特点挑选合适的工作，向面试官完美地展现自己。如果面试官问到个人性格上的弱点时，最好不要回避这个问题，因为每个人都有弱点。具体做法是：先承认弱点，同时表示会努力改进。

典型问题

What kind of person do you think you are?

你觉得自己是一个什么样的人？

相似问题

1. What kind of character do you have? /What kind of personality do you think you have?
你认为自己的性格是什么样的？
2. How would your friends or teachers describe you?
你的朋友和老师怎样评价你？

3. What is your strongest trait?
你最大的优点是什么？

4. Do you have any weakness (at work)?
你（在工作中）有什么缺点？

Words and Phrases	必备词汇
personality [pɜːsə'nælɪtɪ] n. 个性；品格 character ['kærəktə] n. 性格，品质；角色 trait [treɪt] n. 特性，特点；品质 strength [streŋθ] n. 力量；长处 weakness [wiːknəs] n. 弱点；嗜好 approach [ə'prəʊtʃ] n. 方法；vt. 着手处理 enthusiastically [ɪnˌθjuːzɪ'æstɪkəlɪ] adv. 热心地；满腔热情地 nervous ['nɜːvəs] n. 紧张不安的 concentrate ['kɒns(ə)ntreɪt] on 专注于…… outward ['aʊtwəd] adj. 向外的 difficulty ['dɪfɪk(ə)ltɪ] n. 困难，困境 exciting [ɪk'saɪtɪŋ; ek-] adj. 令人兴奋的；使人激动的 satisfying ['sætɪsfaɪɪŋ] adj. 令人满意的；令人满足的 content [kən'tent] adj. 满意的 frankly ['fræŋklɪ] adv. 真诚地，坦白地 teamwork ['tiːmwɜːk] n. 团队合作 partner ['pɑːtnə] n. 伙伴；合伙人 interact [ɪntər'ækt] with 互动 colleague ['kɒliːg] n. 同事，同僚 cooperate [kəʊ'ɒpəreɪt] vi. 合作，配合，协助 creative [kriː'eɪtɪv] adj. 有创意的 humorous ['hjuːmərəs] adj. 幽默的 calm [kɑːm] adj. 冷静的 ambitious [æm'bɪʃəs] adj. 雄心勃勃的 reliable [rɪ'laɪəb(ə)l] adj. 可靠的 careful ['keəfl; -f(ə)l] adj. 细心的 careless ['keələs] adj. 粗心的	honest ['ɒnɪst] adj. 诚实的 hardworking ['hɑːdˌwɜːkɪŋ] adj. 努力工作的 responsible [rɪ'spɒnsɪbl] adj. 负责的 qualified ['kwɒlɪfaɪd] adj. 合格的；有资格的 friendly ['fren(d)lɪ] adj. 友好的 sensitive ['sensɪtɪv] adj. 敏感的 caring ['keərɪŋ] adj. 关心他人的 determined [dɪ'tɜːmɪnd] adj. 有决心的 enthusiastic [ɪnˌθjuːzɪ'æstɪk] adj. 热情的 patience ['peɪʃ(ə)ns] n. 耐心；容忍 trifle ['traɪf(ə)l] n. 琐事 possess [pə'zes] vt. 拥有；掌握 characteristic [ˌkærəktə'rɪstɪk] adj. 典型的 n. 特征；特色 confident ['kɒnfɪdənt] adj. 有信心的 overcome [əʊvə'kʌm] v. 克服 client ['klaɪənt] n. 客户；顾客 active ['æktɪv] adj. 积极的 passive ['pæsɪv] adj. 消极的 extroverted ['ekstrəʊvɜːtɪd] adj. 外向的 introverted ['ɪntrə(ʊ)vɜːtɪd] adj. 内向的 energetic [ˌenə'dʒetɪk] adj. 精力充沛 optimistic [ɒptɪ'mɪstɪk] adj. 乐观的 funny ['fʌnɪ] adj. 风趣的 independent [ˌɪndɪ'pendənt] adj. 独立的 motivated ['məʊtɪveɪtɪd] adj. 有动力的 productive [prə'dʌktɪv] adj. 富有成效的 capable ['keɪpəb(ə)l] adj. 有才能的 open ['əʊp(ə)n] adj. 坦率的

Part 2
In an Interview 面试中

Mini Dialogues	**迷你问答**
Q: What kind of personality do you think you have?	Q：你认为你是什么样的人？
A: Well, I approach things very enthusiastically. I don't like to leave something half-done. It makes me nervous. I can't concentrate on something else until the first thing is finished.	A：嗯，我做事非常热心，我不喜欢半途而废，那会令我很紧张。除非第一件事做完，否则我无法专心做别的事。
Q: Do you think you are more outward-looking or more inward-looking?	Q：你认为自己是外向的还是内向的人？
A: I like being around people and doing things with people. So outgoing, I guess.	A：我喜欢在人群中和大家一起做事，所以我想是外向。
Q: How do you get along with others?	Q：你与别人相处得如何？
A: I get on well with others. Wherever I meet with difficulties, they are always ready to lend me a hand.	A：我和别人相处得很好。只要我遇到困难，他们总是愿意伸出援助之手。
Q: What will you do When you have different opionians with someone else?	Q：你和别人有不同意见时会怎么做？
A: I will speak out if I think he's wrong, but if I understand his thoughts and see he has some good ideas, then I will be very happy to go along with him.	A：如果我认为某人的看法不对，我会明确说出来，但是如果我了解他的想法，并且知道他有一些好主意，那么我就会很高兴地赞同他的意见。
Q: Do you like to work with people?	Q：你喜欢与人接触的工作吗？
A: Yes, I love working with people. When I worked in a clothing store, I met and dealt with all kinds of people every day. It was exciting. Everyone is different and I was excited to give suggestions and find the best clothes for each customer. It was satisfying to see the customers leaving the store, content with my choice. I would not be interested in a job that does not give me a chance to interact with people.	A：是的，我喜欢与人接触。当我在服装店工作时，每天都可以接待各种不同的顾客，这让我觉得很开心。每个人都不同，我很高兴能针对不同的顾客给予不同的建议，并为每位顾客找到最适合自己的衣服。看到顾客带着我选择的衣服满意地离开时，我也感到心满意足。所以，对于没有机会与人接触的工作，我不感兴趣。
Q: What are some of you weaknesses and strengths?	Q：你有哪些缺点和优点？
A: Well, I'm afraid I'm a poor talker, and that isn't very good, so I've been studying how to speak in public. I suppose a strong point is that I like developing new things and ideas.	A：我恐怕我不太善于表达，这样不大好，所以我一直在学习如何当众说话。我想我有一个优点那就是我喜欢新事物和提出新想法。

Mini Dialogues	迷你问答
Q: Would you say you have a lot of friends, or just a few? A: Not so many, but not really just a few, either, I suppose. There are about six people that I see quite a bit of now. They're good friends. Q: How would your friends or colleagues describe you? A: They say Lina is an honest, hard-working and responsible person who deeply cares for her family and friends.	Q: 你认为你有很多朋友，还是只有几个？ A: 我想不是很多，但也不是只有几个。我现在经常见面的大概有六个，都是好朋友。 Q: 你的朋友或同事怎样形容你？ A: 他们说莉娜是位诚实、工作努力、有责任心的人，她对家庭和朋友都很关心。

Situational Dialogue 1	实战演习 1
A: What position are you applying for? B: I'm applying for the job as a secretary. A: Why do you think you are qualified for the job? What kind of person do you think you are? B: I am a friendly, sensitive, caring and determined person. A: For this position, the most important trait is being enthusiastic and having patience in dealing with trifles. B: I possess these traits. I'm the right person for this job.	A: 你应聘什么职位？ B: 我应聘秘书一职。 A: 你为什么觉得你能胜任这份工作？你觉得自己是一个什么样的人？ B: 我是个很友善、敏感、关心他人和有上进心的人。 A: 对于这个岗位而言，最重要的品质是对要处理的琐事保持热心和耐心。 B: 我认为我具备这样的特点。我适合这份工作。

Situational Dialogue 2	实战演习 2
A: Do you have the personal characteristics necessary for success in your chosen career? B: Well, I think so. I am confident and easygoing. Those are my strongest personalities. Because I am confident, I can overcome all kinds of difficulties. I am easygoing, so I can work well with my colleagues. Besides, my clients will like to communicate with me.	A: 你具有胜任这份工作所要求的性格特点吗？ B: 哦，我认为是的。我很自信，而且性格随和，这是我最重要的性格特点。因为自信，我能克服一切困难。随和的性格使我能和同事们融洽地工作，并且客户也会因此喜欢和我交流。

Part 2
In an Interview 面试中

续

Situational Dialogue 2	实战演习 2
A: Then what kind of person would you like to work with? B: Generally speaking, I can work well with all kinds of people, but frankly speaking, I would like to work in a team. In my opinion, teamwork is the key to success, so those who can work as a part of a team will be my best partners. A: You would like to work in a team, then would you like to be a leader or a follower in a team? B: Everyone is important in a team. The most important thing is that we can cooperate well with each other and everyone will try their best, then the team will be successful.	A：那么你喜欢和什么样的人一起工作呢？ B：一般说来，我和各类人都能很好地一起工作。但坦率地讲，我喜欢在团队里工作。在我看来，团队合作是成功的关键。所以，有团队意识的人将会是我的好搭档。 A：你想在一个团队里工作，那么，你想成为这个团队里的领导者还是追随者呢？ B：在团队里每个人都很重要。最重要的是我们能很好地合作，每个人都竭尽全力。这样我们的团队才会成功。

练习

1. What kind of person do you think you are?

....
....
....
....

2. What kind of character do you have?

....
....
....
....

3. What is your strongest trait?

....
....

4. Do you have any weakness (at work)?

轻松一刻

A Joke

Patient: Tell me, doctor. Are there any chances for me to recover?

Doctor: Just 100 percent! Statistics show that only nine out of ten die from your disease and nine of my patients have already died from it. You're the tenth!

Lesson 6　Hobbies and Interests
兴趣与爱好

章节说明

求职者不要以为谈论兴趣爱好是轻松的话题，实际上，面试官是想知道你是否有激情，懂得劳逸结合，有时间和精力去参加丰富多彩的活动。同时兴趣也会反映一个人是外向型性格还是创新型性格，是否有毅力，是否精力充沛等。

求职者不要一口气说出一大堆兴趣爱好，那样有可能让面试官怀疑你是否还有时间集中精力工作。可以适度地列举几个兴趣爱好，证明自己精力充沛、博学多才。

典型问题

What are your interests outside work?
你工作之余的兴趣是什么？

相似问题

1. Do you have any special interests outside your work?
除了工作，你还有其他特别的爱好吗？
2. What do you do on weekend?
你周末一般干什么？
3. How do you entertain yourself after work?
工作之余你有哪些娱乐活动？
4. What do you usually do for fun in your leisure time?
你在业余时间通常有哪些娱乐活动？

Words and Phrases 必备词汇

hobby ['hɒbɪ] *n.* 业余爱好
interest ['ɪnt(ə)rɪst] *n.* 兴趣
entertain [entə'teɪn] *vt.* 娱乐
leisure ['leʒə] *n.* 空闲，闲暇
listening to music ['mjuːzɪk] *n.* 音乐
do sports= play sports 运动
jogging ['dʒɒgɪŋ] *n.* 慢跑
photography [fə'tɒɪgrəfɪ] *n.* 摄影
favorite ['feɪvərɪt] *adj.* 喜欢的；*n.* 喜欢的人和事
play football/basketball 踢足球 / 打篮球
musical instrument ['ɪnstrʊm(ə)nt] 乐器
play the piano [pɪ'ænəʊ] 弹钢琴
swimming 游泳
library ['laɪbrərɪ] *n.* 图书馆
literary ['lɪt(ə)(rə)rɪ] *adj.* 文学的
classic ['klæsɪk] *adj.* 经典的；古典的 *n.* 经典著作
reciting [rɪ'saɪtɪŋ] poems ['pəʊɪmz] 背诵诗歌
playing computer games 玩电脑游戏
playing card/chess 打牌 / 下棋
dancing 舞蹈
go skiing ['skiːɪŋ] 滑雪
keeping pets 养宠物
rafting ['ræftɪŋ] 漂流
diving ['daɪvɪŋ] 潜水

benefit from 从……中获益
planting flowers 种花
flying kites 放风筝
walking a pet dog 遛狗
singing 唱歌
watching movies 看电影
skating 溜冰
roller skating 轮滑
fishing 钓鱼
climbing mountains 登山
painting 绘画
acting 表演
collecting coins 搜集硬币
collecting stamps 集邮
making model planes 制作航模
hiking ['haɪkɪŋ] *n.* 徒步旅行
reading novels ['nɒɪv(ə)lz] 读小说
horseback riding 骑马
mini-blogging writing 写微博
cooking ['kʊkɪŋ] *n.* 烹饪
badminton ['bædmɪnt(ə)n] *n.* 羽毛球
volleyball ['vɒlɪbɔːl] *n.* 排球
tennis/table tennis ['tenɪs] 网球 / 乒乓球
taichi 太极拳
DIY design [dɪ'zaɪn] 手工设计
cross stitch [stɪtʃ] 十字绣

Part 2
In an Interview 面试中

续

Words and Phrases	必备词汇
surfing ['sɜːfɪŋ] 冲浪 surfing on line 上网 rowing 划船 bowling ['bəʊlɪŋ] 保龄球 gardening 园艺 camping ['kæmpɪŋ] n. 露营	high / long jump 跳高 / 跳远 guitar [gɪ'tɑː] n. 吉他 violin [vaɪə'lɪn] n. 小提琴 drama ['drɑːmə] n. 喜剧 / 剧本 aerobic [eə'rəʊbɪk] exercise 有氧运动 travel ['træv(ə)l] n. 旅行；v. 旅行

Mini Dialogues	迷你问答
Q: Do you have any special interests outside your work? A: Yes, I like listening to music after work. Q: What do you do on weekend? A: I usually stay at home and have a good rest. Q: How do you entertain yourself after work? A: I enjoy doing sports and I love jogging. Q: What do you usually do for fun in your leisure time? A: I usually take photos in my leisure time. Photography can not only take my mind off my work but also make me keep the perfect moments. Q: Do you have any favorite sports? A: There is nothing I like more than football. Q: What musical instruments do you play? A: I can play the piano a bit. Q: What do you think is the most important thing for you to be happy? A: I think that the most important thing is having good friends. A person can't live all by himself. It takes a lot of people working and cooperating together. The more really close friends I have, the better I would become.	Q：除了工作，你还有其他特别的兴趣爱好吗？ A：有，下班后我喜欢听音乐。 Q：你周末一般干什么？ A：我通常待在家，好好休息。 Q：工作之余你有哪些娱乐活动？ A：我喜欢运动，我喜爱慢跑。 Q：你在业余时间通常有哪些娱乐活动？ A：我经常摄影。摄影不但可以把我的注意力从工作中转移出来，而且也能让我留住美好的瞬间。 Q：你有特别喜欢的运动吗？ A：没有什么比足球更让我喜欢了。 Q：你会弹奏什么乐器？ A：我会一点钢琴。 Q：你认为能让你快乐的最重要的事情是什么？ A：我认为最重要的是要有好朋友。一个人不能独立生活，要有很多人一起工作和合作，所以好朋友越多，我也会越优秀。

酒店面试英语

Situational Dialogue 1	实战演习 1
A: How do you entertain yourself after work? B: I like doing sports. A: What kind of sports do you like best? B: I especially like swimming. A: Why? B: It helps me to keep fit and I enjoy the feeling in the water like a fish.	A：工作之余你会进行哪些娱乐活动？ B：我喜欢运动。 A：你最喜欢哪种运动？ B：我喜欢游泳。 A：为什么？ B：游泳有助于我保持身体健康，另外我喜欢在水中的感觉，像鱼一样。

Situational Dialogue 2	实战演习 2
A: What do you usually do on weekend? B: I usually read books at home or in the library. I'm a bookworm. A: What kinds of books do you like to read? B: I especially like to read literary classics. A: Do you benefit from reading? B: Definitely, reading makes me realize life is more colorful and changeable.	A：周末你一般干什么？ B：我通常在家或在图书馆读书。我是一个书虫。 A：你喜欢读什么类型的书？ B：我特别喜欢读经典文学作品。 A：你从阅读中是否有所受益？ B：当然，阅读让我意识到生活很多彩也很多变。

练习

1. Do you have any special interests outside your work?
   ....
   ....
   ....
   ....

2. What do you do on weekend?
   ....
   ....
   ....

Part 2 In an Interview 面试中

....
....

3. Do you have any favorite sports?

....
....
....
....

4. What kinds of books do you like to read?

....
....
....
....

轻松一刻

A Joke

Jack: Mum, when I grow up, I want to be an Arctic explorer.
Mother: That's fine, Jack.
Jack: But I want to go into training at once.
Mother: How so?
Jack: Well, I want a dollar a day for ice-cream, so I'll get used to the cold.

Lesson 7　College Life 大学生活

章节说明

对于应届毕业生来说，教育背景和校园生活的介绍在面试中至关重要。在回答这部分的问题时，求职者不必面面俱到，应该根据职位要求，重点介绍相关内容，如参加的比赛、活动、加入的社团、学生会等，在其中所任职务或承担的工作、责任等，使面试官认识到你就是他要找的人。

典型问题

Why did you take Hotel Management as your major?
你为什么选择酒店管理作为你的专业？

相似问题

1. What made you decide to study Hotel Management?
你为什么要学习酒店管理？

Part 2 In an Interview 面试中

2. How do you comment on your behavior in the college life?
你怎么评价你在大学里的表现？

3. How were your grades at college?
你读大学时成绩如何？

4. Did you take any position in college?
你在大学期间担任过什么职务吗？

5. Have you got any special experience during your college life?
在你的大学生活中，有什么特别的经历吗？

Words and Phrases 必备词汇

college ['kɔilɪdʒ] n. 大学，学院
major ['meɪdʒə] n. 主修科目 adj. 主要的
comment ['kɔiment] n. 评论；意见 vi. 发表评论
behavior [bɪheɪvjə] n. 行为，举止
position [pə'zɪʃən] n. 职位，职务
experience [ɪk'spɪərɪəns; ek-] n.&v. 经验，经历
grant [grɑːnt] vt. 授予；允许；承认
specialty ['speʃ(ə)ltɪ] n. 专业
decision [dɪ'sɪʒ(ə)n] n. 决定，决心；决议
excellent ['eksələnt] adj. 卓越的，杰出的
frontier ['frʌntɪə; frʌn'tɪə] n. 前沿，边界；adj. 边界的；开拓的
contribute [kən'trɪbjut] to 贡献
international [ɪntə'næʃənəl] adj. 国际的
required [rɪ'kwaɪəd] adj. 必须的
professor [prə'fesə] n. 教授
minor ['maɪnə] n. 辅修科目
subject ['sʌbdʒekt] n. 科目
course [kɔːs] n. 科目；课程
required/compulsory [kəm'pʌls(ə)rɪ] course 必修课
optional ['ɔpʃ(ə)n(ə)l] /elective [ɪ'lektɪv] course 选修课

economy [ɪ'kɔinəmɪ] n. 经济
professional [prə'feʃənəl] adj. 专业的；n. 专业人士
hard-working [hɑːd 'wəːkɪŋ] adj. 勤奋的，努力工作的
grade [greɪd] n. 年级；等级；成绩
Banquet ['bæŋkwɪt] Planning and Design 宴会策划与设计
President of the Student Union ['juːnjən] 学生会主席
performance [pə'fɔːm(ə)ns] n. 表现
university [juːnɪ'vɜːsɪtɪ] n.（综合性）大学
institute ['ɪnstɪtjuːt] n. 学会，学院
department [dɪ'pɑːtm(ə)nt] n. 部门，系，科
president ['prezɪd(ə)nt] n.（大学）校长
dean [diːn] n. 院长；系主任
Operation and Management in Food and Beverage ['bev(ə)rɪdʒ] Department 餐饮经营与管理
Western Bakery ['beɪk(ə)rɪ] and Pastry ['peɪstrɪ] 西点制作
Food Nutrition [njʊ'trɪʃ(ə)n] and Hygiene ['haɪdʒiːn] 食品营养卫生
Decoration [ˌdekə'reɪʃ(ə)n] Design [dɪ'zaɪn] in Hotel Industry 酒店装饰设计

续

Words and Phrases	必备词汇
curriculum（复数 curricular）[kə'rɪkjʊləm] n. 课程 Hotel English 酒店英语 Business Etiquette ['etɪket; etɪ'ket] 商务礼仪 Hotel Management 酒店管理 Consumer Psychology [saɪ'kɒlədʒɪ] 消费心理学 Tourists' Countries Profile ['prəʊfaɪl] 客源国概况 Secretary in Hotel Industry 酒店文秘 Financial [faɪ'nænʃ(ə)l] Management in Hotel Industry 酒店财务管理 Principles ['prɪnsəplz] of Management 管理学原理 Public Relations in Hotel Industry 酒店公共关系 Laws and Regulations [ˌregjʊ'leɪʃ(ə)nz] in Hotel Industry 酒店法律与法规 Applied [ə'plaɪd] Economics [iːkə'nɒmɪks; ek-] 应用经济学 Operation [ɒpə'reɪʃ(ə)n] and Management in Front Office Department 前厅经营与管理 Chinese Food Culture 中国饮食文化 Cocktails ['kɒkteɪl] Making and Presenting [prɪ'zent] 鸡尾酒调制 academic [ækə'demɪk] adj. 学术的；理论的；学院的 evaluation [ɪˌvælju'eɪʃn] n. 评价 score [skɔː] n. 分数 credit ['kredɪt] n. 信用；贷款；学分 reward [rɪ'wɔːd] n. 报酬，奖励 certificate [sə'tɪfɪkɪt] n. 证书 scholarship ['skɒləʃɪp] n. 奖学金 Excellent Student 三好学生 excellent class cadre ['kɑːdə] 优秀班干部	Operation and Management in Housekeeping Department 客房经营与管理 Wine Knowledge and Bar Management 酒水与酒吧管理 Hotel Marketing ['mɑːkɪtɪŋ] 酒店市场营销 Facility [fə'sɪləti] Management in Hotel Industry 酒店设备管理 Operation and Management in Recreation [ˌrekrɪ'eɪʃ(ə)n] and Entertainment [entə'teɪnm(ə)nt] Department 康乐经营与管理 Supervision [ˌsuːpə'vɪʒn] Management in Hotel Industry 酒店督导管理 Star-rating ['reɪtɪŋ] Standards ['stændəd] in Hotel Industry 酒店星级标准解读 Improvement [ɪm'pruːvm(ə)nt] of Vocational [və(ʊ)'keɪʃ(ə)n(ə)l] Aptitude ['æptɪtjuːd] in Hotel Industry 酒店职业能力提升 The Art of Flower Arrangement [ə'reɪn(d)ʒm(ə)nt] 插花艺术 Director of Sports Department, the Student Union 学生会体育部部长 General Affairs [ə'feəz] Department 生活部 Publicity [pʌb'lɪsɪtɪ] Department 宣传部 Study Department 学习部 Communist ['kɒmjʊnɪst] Youth League Committee [kə'mɪtɪ] 院团委 Students' Association [əˌsəʊsɪ'eɪʃ(ə)n] / Society / Club 学生会，学生社团 volunteer [ˌvɒlən'tɪə] activity [æk'tɪvɪtɪ] 志愿者活动 extracurricular [ˌekstrəkə'rɪkjʊlə] adj. 课外的；业余的

Part 2
In an Interview 面试中

Mini Dialogues	迷你问答
Q: Why did you choose to attend Zhengzhou Tourism College?	Q：你为什么选择郑州旅游职业学院？
A: I chose ZTC because Hotel Management department was granted as national key specialty. I'm happy with my decision. I received the excellent and frontier education possible and I'm confident that I have the knowledge and skills, so I can readily contribute to your hotel.	A：我选择郑州旅院的原因是，我们学院的酒店管理专业是国家级重点专业。我非常满意自己的决定。我接受了优秀而前沿的教育，并对自己拥有的知识和技能充满自信，随时可以为贵酒店做出贡献。
Q: What is your major?	Q：你的专业是什么？
A: Hotel Management.	A：酒店管理。
Q: Why did you take Hotel Management as your major?	Q：你为什么选择酒店管理专业？
A: I took Hotel Management as my major because I always want to work in an international hotel. Besides I like communicating with people.	A：我选择酒店管理作为我的专业，是因为我一直想在一家国际性的酒店工作。而且我喜欢与人交流。
Q: Which college class did you like best? Why?	Q：你最喜欢学校的哪门课程？为什么？
A: I like Hotel English best. I think it is very interesting. English is the language in the global market place. As our economy becomes increasingly global, I think English is the basic skill that is required for almost any professional.	A：我最喜欢酒店英语。我觉得它很有意思。英语是全球市场的通用语言。随着我们的经济日益全球化，我认为英语是一项基本技能，几乎每个专业人士都需要掌握。
Q: How do you comment on your behavior in the college life?	Q：你怎么评价自己在大学时的表现？
A: Generally speaking, I did an excellent job in my college life. I am active and hard-working.	A：总的来说，我在大学里表现很好。我很积极，也很努力。
Q: How were your grades at college?	Q：你读大学时成绩如何？
A: Not bad. In *Banquet Planning and Design*, I even got 90 points, I remember.	A：还不错。我记得《宴会策划与设计》这门课，我还得了90分。

Mini Dialogues	迷你问答
Q: Did you take any position in college? A: No, I didn't. In fact, I spent my whole time on studying. Q: Have you got any special experience during your college life? A: I was the president of the Student Union and I learned a lot.	Q: 你在大学期间担任过什么职务吗? A: 没有。实际上,我把所有的时间都投入到了学习中。 Q: 在你的大学生活中,有什么特别的经历吗? A: 我曾是学生会主席,学到了不少东西。

Situational Dialogue 1	实战演习 1
A: How do you comment on your behavior in your college life? B: Generally speaking, I did an excellent job in my college life. A: What about your performance in working? B: I am energetic and hard-working. A: So, which do you prefer, studying in college or working in a company? B: I think I prefer working.	A: 你怎么评价自己在大学时的表现? B: 总的来说,我在大学里表现很好。 A: 那你的工作表现怎么样? B: 我精力充沛,也很勤奋。 A: 你更喜欢上学还是工作? B: 我想我更喜欢工作。

Situational Dialogue 2	实战演习 2
A: Where did you graduate from, Qiao? B: I graduated from Zhengzhou Tourism College. A: What's your major? B: My major is Hotel Management. A: Considering your major, I think you must be good at communicating with people? B: Yes, I have excellent communication skill.	A: 乔,你是哪所学校毕业的? B: 我毕业于郑州旅游职业学院。 A: 你的专业是什么? B: 我的专业是酒店管理。 A: 考虑到你的专业,你肯定很善于与人沟通吧? B: 是的,我具备出色的沟通技能。

Part 2
In an Interview 面试中

练习

1. Why did you choose to attend Zhengzhou Tourism College?

2. Why did you take Hotel Management as your major?

3. Which curriculum did you like the best? Why?

4. How do you comment on your behavior in your college life?

5. Have you got any special experience during your college life?

酒店面试英语

轻松一刻

Lesson 8　Working Experience　工作经验

章节说明

求职者在讲述自己的工作经验时应多提及与应聘职位相关的工作经验。根据职位的要求，突出能体现职位需要的工作经验或职位需要的个人素质。求职者也可告诉面试官自己在工作中所学到的工作方法和技巧，来体现自己的学习能力。若碰到比较负面的问题，应尽量避免用批判的语气来回答，要以积极的态度来回应此类问题。在回答中，应实话实说，注意自己的语气和表情。

典型问题

Do you have any working experience?
你有工作经验吗？

相似问题

1. Did you do any part-time job while in college?
你在大学期间做过兼职工作吗？

酒店面试英语

2. How does your work experience relate to this job?
你的工作经历与这个职位有什么样的联系？
3. What have you gained from your part-time job?
你从兼职工作经历中有什么收获？

Words and Phrases	**必备词汇**
part-time *adj.* 兼职的 relate to 涉及，有关 gain from 从……获得利益 secretary ['sekrətri] *n.* 秘书；干事 learn from 向……学习 boss [bɔis] *n.* 老板，上司 professional [prə'feʃənl] *adj.* 专业的 employer [ɪm'plɔiə; em-] *n.* 雇主，老板 dependable [dɪ'pendəbl] *adj.* 可靠的 employee [emplɔi'i:] *n.* 雇员 boring ['bɔ:rɪŋ] *adj.* 无聊的 pizza ['pi:tsə] *n.* 比萨饼	hut [hʌt] *n.* 小屋；临时营房 register ['redʒɪstə] *vt.* 登记；注册 *n.* 注册；寄存器；登记簿 conference ['kɔinf(ə)r(ə)ns] *n.* 会议 tough [tʌf] *adj.* 艰苦的，困难的；坚强的，不屈不挠的 focused ['fəʊkəst] *adj.* 聚焦的；专心的 search [sɜ:tʃ] *v.* 搜扑；调查；探求 website ['websaɪt] *n.* 网站 full-time *adj.* 专职的；全日制的 temporary ['temp(ə)rəri] *adj.* 暂时的，临时的

Mini Dialogues	**迷你问答**
Q：Do you have working experience? A：I used to work as a secretary. Q：What did you enjoy most about your last job? A：I loved interacting with customers. It was exciting to deal with all kinds of people. Q：What did you enjoy least about your last job? A：I really like my job, so I can't think of anything major I disliked. Q：What have you learned from your past jobs? A：I have learned a lot about serving the guests and basic office skills.	Q：你有工作经验吗？ A：我曾经是一名秘书。 Q：在上一份工作中，你最喜欢哪方面？ A：我喜欢与顾客交流。能够与各种各样的人接触，我感到非常高兴。 Q：在上一份工作中，你最不喜欢哪方面？ A：我非常喜欢我的工作，所以我想不出有什么不太喜欢的事。 Q：从过去的工作中，你学到了什么？ A：我学会了很多为客人服务和基本的办公室工作的技能。

Part 2
In an Interview 面试中

续

Mini Dialogues	迷你问答
Q: What do you think of your boss? A: My boss had a kind personality and he was very professional. Q: Have you taken any part-time jobs when you were at college? A: Yes, of course. I have worked in a restaurant for two years. Q: What was your last employer's opinion of you? A: My last boss said I was a very responsible and dependable employee. Q: What is the most boring job you've ever had? A: I don't really think I've ever had a boring job. Each job was a great experience for a college student.	Q：你认为你的上司如何？ A：我的老板性格和善，而且他非常专业。 Q：你在大学时有没有从事过兼职工作？ A：当然做过。我在一家餐馆工作了两年。 Q：上一个雇主对你的评价如何？ A：我之前的上司说我是一位有责任感而且值得信赖的员工。 Q：你曾做过的最无聊的工作是什么？ A：我觉得过去没有哪些工作很无聊。每份工作对一个大学生而言都是一次非常棒的经历。

Situational Dialogue 1	实战演习 1
A: Did you have a part-time job when you were still in college? B: Yeah, I worked about twenty hours a week in Pizza Hut. A: What was that like? B: It was always very busy there. A: What did you do? B: I stood behind the register and took pizza orders. A: What have you learned from your past jobs? B: I have learned about how to serve the guests and the use of Microsoff settlement system.	A：你读书期间有没有兼职工作的经验？ B：有过。我在一家必胜客比萨店每周工作20个小时。 A：工作怎么样？ B：那儿总是很忙。 A：你在那儿负责做什么呢？ B：我站在收银台后面接单。 A：从过去的工作中，你学到了什么？ B：我学会了如何为客人服务和操作微软结账系统。

65

Situational Dialogue 2

A: What have you ever taken as part-time jobs when you were in college?

B: When I was in college, I worked as a volunteer for the conferences held in our college.

A: What would you say about the part-time job?

B: As for my part-time job, it was really a tough one and I had to stay focused all the time.

A: Why did you have to be focused all the time?

B: If I was not focused, I would make mistakes.

A: Yes, that was really tough. How did you find that job?

B: I just searched on the website of my college.

实战演习 2

A：你在大学的时候有没有从事过什么兼职工作？

B：大学时，我作为一名志愿者在我院举办的众多会议上工作。

A：你会如何评价你的兼职工作？

B：说到我的兼职工作，它真的很辛苦，我需要时刻保持注意力集中。

A：为什么时刻都要保持注意力集中呢？

B：如果我不时刻保持注意力，我就会出错。

A：是的，这确实很辛苦。你是怎样找到这份工作的？

B：我在学校网站上搜索到的。

练习

1. Do you have working experience?

2. What have you learned from your past jobs?

轻松一刻

The New Teacher

George comes from school on the first of September.

"George, how did you like your new teacher?" asked his mother.

"I didn't like her, mother, because she said that three and three were six and then she said that two and four were six too..."

Lesson 9　Strengths 求职优势

章节说明

如果你是应届毕业生，在没有工作经验的情况下，应该说明自己有哪些长处可以应用在工作上，并结合对方所要求的能力或技术进行详细说明。企业特别重视讲诚信、有干劲，具有主动性、协作性、执行力和沟通能力的人。切勿过分夸大自己的优势，以免给人留下不诚恳的印象。

典型问题

What are some of your strengths?
你有哪些优点？

相似问题

1. What's your strongest point?
你的强项是什么？

Part 2
In an Interview 面试中

2. Do you have any strong points?
你有什么强项吗？
3. What are your advantages?
你的优势是什么？

Words and Phrases / 必备词汇

strength [streŋθ] *n.* 力量；优点，长处
strong/weak point 强项 / 弱点
advantag [əd'vɑ:ntɪdʒ] *n.* 优势
disadvantage [ˌdɪsəd'vɑ:ntɪdʒ] *n.* 缺点
stress-resistant [stres rɪ'zɪstənt] *adj.* 抗压的
shorthand ['ʃɔ:thænd] *n.* 速记；速记法
fluency ['flu:ənsɪ] *n.*（语言、文章）流利；（技能）娴熟
patient ['peɪʃnt] *adj.* 有耐心的
license ['laɪsns] *n.* 执照，许可证
self-controlling 自控

interpersonal [ˌɪntə'pɜ:snl] *adj.* 人际的
competence ['kɔmpɪt(ə)ns] *n.* 能力
persuade [pə'sweɪd] *v.* 说服
recruit [rɪ'kru:t] *v.&n.* 招聘
clerk [klɑ:k] *n.* 职员
apply [ə'plaɪ] for 申请，请求
inform [ɪn'fɔ:m] of 通知；报告
weakness ['wi:knəs] *n.* 弱点，软弱；嗜好
self-adjusting [ˌselfə'dʒʌstɪŋ] *adj.&n.* 自我调整
self-development 自我发展

Mini Dialogues / 迷你问答

Q：What are some of your strengths?
A：I'm highly stress-resistant.
Q：What's your strongest point?
A：I have excellent people skills.
Q：What's your greatest strength?
A：I think I am good at planning.
Q：Do you have any special skills?
A：Yes, I take shorthand pretty fast.
Q：How is your language ability?
A：I believe my English is quite fluent.
Q：Can you manage English conversation?
A：Yes, I'm sure I can.
Q：What are your advantages?
A：I am careful and patient in doing things.
Q：Do you have any licenses?
A：Yes, I have a driver's license.
Q：What advantages do you have ?
A：I am good at self-controlling.

Q：你认为自己有哪些优势？
A：我的抗压能力很强。
Q：你的强项是什么？
A：我的社交能力很好。
Q：你最大的优势是什么？
A：我认为我很擅长计划。
Q：你有什么特殊技能吗？
A：有，我的速记很快。
Q：你的语言能力怎么样？
A：我认为自己的英语相当流利。
Q：你能用英语交谈吗？
A：是的，当然可以。
Q：你的优势是什么？
A：我做事情耐心仔细。
Q：你有什么执照吗？
A：有，我有驾驶执照。
Q：你认为自己有什么优势？
A：我有很强的自控能力。

酒店面试英语

Situational Dialogue 1	实战演习 1
A：What would you say is your greatest strength? B：I am a fast learner. A：Do you think you are a good employee? B：Generally speaking, I would say yes. My interpersonal competences are very good. My greatest skill is that I am good at persuading the clients to accept our points. A：Do you think you still need some improvement? B：Yes, I need to try harder in language study.	A：你认为你最大的优点是什么？ B：我学习东西很快。 A：你觉得自己是个有能力的员工吗？ B：总体来说，我的回答是肯定的。我的人际交往能力不错。我最强的能力是说服客户接受我们的观点。 A：你觉得自己还有什么需要改进吗？ B：是的。我应该加强外语学习。

Situational Dialogue 2	实战演习 2
A：I heard that your hotel is recruiting a reservation clerk. I want to apply for this position. B：OK, do you have any strong points? A：My strength is that I'm independent when dealing with trifles. B：Are you good at communicating with people? A：Yes, I am good at communicating with others. B：I will inform you of the result in three days.	A：我听说贵酒店要招聘一位预订部职员。我想申请这个职位。 B：好的。您有什么特长吗？ A：我的优点是我可以独立处理琐事。 B：您擅长与人打交道吗？ A：是的，我很擅长与人沟通。 B：我会在三天内通知你结果。

练习

1. What is your greatest strength?

　　..
　　..

Part 2
In an Interview 面试中

2. Can you speak English fluently?

轻松一刻

A Joke

Linda: I have some problem with my new computer.
Leo: What's wrong?
Linda: It's telling me to press any key to continue. But where is the "any" key?

71

Lesson 10 Jobs and Positions
应聘职位

章节说明

求职者如被问及此类问题，应意识到这是一个能够展示自己对应聘职位或者企业有多了解的好机会。求职者应对应聘职位有所了解，掌握其工作内容、职位要求等。对于心仪的职位，应具体叙述与其相关的学习或工作经验。

典型问题

Why are you interested in this job?
你为什么对这份工作感兴趣？

相似问题

1. Why do you want to work for our hotel?
你为什么选择在我们酒店工作？

2. What made you decide to stay here?
你为什么选择留在这里？

3. Do you know anything about the position?
你了解这个职位吗？

Words and Phrases	必备词汇
position [pə'zɪʃ(ə)n] n. 位置，方位；职位	staff [stɑːf] n. 职员
post [pəʊst] n. 岗位	pleasure ['pleʒə] n. 快乐；令人高兴的事
suitable ['sjuːtəbl] adj. 合适的，适当的	resume ['rezjumeɪ] n. 简历 [rɪ'zjuːm] vt. 重新开始
cherish ['tʃerɪʃ] vt. 怀有（感情等）；抱有（希望等）	be aware [ə'weə] of 知道，意识到
desire [dɪ'zaɪə] v./n. 希望	aspect ['æspekt] n. 方面
expect [ɪk'spekt; ek-] v. 期望	research [rɪ'sɜːtʃ] n.&v. 研究；调查
qualification [ˌkwɒlɪfɪ'keɪʃ(ə)n] n. 资格；资历	section ['sekʃ(ə)n] n. 部分；部门
relevant ['reləvənt] adj. 相关的	Fitness Center 健身中心
knowhow [nəʊhɑʊ] n. 诀窍；实际的能力；专门技术	salary ['sæləri] n. 薪水，薪金
attendant [ə'tend(ə)nt] n. 服务员	working hours 工作时间
come across v. 偶遇；无意中发现	fixed [fɪkst] adj. 确定的
advertisement [əd'vɜːtɪzm(ə)nt] n. 广告，宣传	on average ['æv(ə)rɪdʒ] 平均；普通，通常
receptionist [rɪ'sepʃ(ə)nɪst] n. 接待员	depend on 取决于
be fit for 适合（于），对……合适；胜任	shift [ʃɪft] n. 移动；变化；轮班
spoken English 英语口语	career objective 职业目标
foreigner ['fɒrɪnə] n. 外地人，外国人	Training Department 培训部
advanced [əd'vɑːnst] adj. 先进的	Accounting [ə'kaʊntɪŋ] Department 财务部
Front Office Department [dɪ'pɑːtm(ə)nt] 前厅部	Sales & Marketing Department 市场营销部
Food & Beverage ['bev(ə)rɪdʒ] Department 餐饮部	Engineering [ˌendʒɪ'nɪərɪŋ] & Maintenance ['meɪnt(ə)nəns] Department 工程部
Human Resources [rɪ'sɔːsɪz] Department 人力资源部	Security [sɪ'kjʊərɪtɪ] Department 保安部
Purchasing ['pɜːtʃəsɪŋ] Department 采购部	Recreation [ˌrekrɪ'eɪʃ(ə)n] Department 康乐部

Mini Dialogues	迷你问答
Q: Why are you interested in this job?	Q：你为什么对这份工作感兴趣？
A: I think I'm quite suitable for it, because my major would be of great use for the job.	A：我认为自己适合这份工作，因为我能将自己所学到的专业知识运用到工作中去。

Mini Dialogues	迷你问答
Q: Why do you choose ABC hotel? A: As you may know, I majored in Hotel Management in college. I've cherished a desire to get a job where I can apply my knowledge. Q: What type of work will you expect to do? A: I wish to do accounting. Q: What qualifications do you have that relate to the position? A: As a Hotel Management major student, I have successfully learned relevant hotel knowhow and management skills. Q: Are you applying for the position of room attendant? A: Yes, that's right. Q: Are you able to take this job? A: I'm sure I can. Q: Are you interested in this position? A: Yes, of course.	Q: 你为什么选择 ABC 酒店？ A: 如你所知，我大学时主修酒店管理，我一直希望得到一份能应用自己所学知识的工作。 Q: 你希望做什么类型的工作？ A: 我希望做会计工作。 Q: 你拥有哪些与这个职位相关的资质？ A: 作为一名酒店管理专业的学生，我已经学到了不少相关知识及管理技能。 Q: 你申请的是客房服务员的职位吗？ A: 是的。 Q: 你能胜任这份工作吗？ A: 是的，当然可以。 Q: 你对这个职位感兴趣吗？ A: 是的，当然。

Situational Dialogue 1	实战演习 1
A: Good morning. Can I help you? B: Yes. I came across your advertisement for receptionists in the newspaper last week. A: Oh, yes. Won't you sit down? What's your name? B: My name is Aaron Zhao. A: Good. May I ask why you are interested in working at our hotel? B: Because I think I'm fit for a receptionist's job. I'm quite fluent in English. I know, your hotel has a lot of foreign guest. What I really want is to learn some advanced methods of management from foreign staff members.	A: 早上好。有什么需要帮助吗？ B: 是的。我看到了上周贵酒店刊登在报纸上的关于前台接待员的招聘广告，我想来试试。 A: 哦，这样啊。请坐。你叫什么名字？ B: 我叫亚伦·赵。 A: 好的。我能否了解一下你为什么想在我们酒店上班呢？ B: 因为我认为自己能胜任前台接待员的工作。我英语口语流利。我知道贵酒店有很多外国客人。我想在此工作的原因还在于想从外国同事那里学到先进的管理方法。

Part 2 In an Interview 面试中

续

Situational Dialogue 1

A: Thank you for your interest in our hotel, Mr. Zhao. Good luck to you.
B: It's my pleasure.

实战演习 1

A：赵先生，谢谢你对我们酒店感兴趣。祝你好运。
B：这是我的荣幸。

Situational Dialogue 2

A: I see by your resume that you have been working.
B: Yes, I have worked for two years with an American company.
A: Are you aware of any aspects of this position and do you feel you are qualified?
B: Yes, I understand my qualification and your needs by researching your company.
A: What starting salary do you expect?
B: I'd like to start at ￥3500 a month.
A: OK. Do you have any questions you would like to ask me?
B: What are the company's working hours?
A: It's not fixed for different departments, on average each day is 8 hours, which depends on your shifts.
B: Thanks.

实战演习 2

A：从你的简历可以看出你一直在工作。
B：是的，我在一家美国公司工作过2年。
A：你对这个职位了解吗？你认为自己能胜任吗？
B：是的，通过对贵公司的研究，我了解了你们的工作要求，并认为我能胜任这个岗位。
A：你想要多少起薪？
B：我想要每月3500元。
A：好的。你还有什么问题要问我吗？
B：公司的上下班时间是怎样的？
A：不同部门上班时间不是固定的，平均每天8个小时，也取决于你的班次。
B：谢谢。

练习

1. What qualifications do you have that relate to the position?

2. Did you learn anything that could be used in a hotel?

轻松一刻

What's worse than finding a worm in your apple?

Finding half a worm in your apple

Lesson 11　Career Planning 职业生涯规划

章节说明

职业生涯规划 (career planning) 是指个人与组织相结合，在对一个人职业生涯的主客观条件进行测定、分析、总结的基础上，再结合时代特点，根据自己的职业抱负，确定出最佳的职业目标，并为实现这一目标做出行之有效的计划。职业规划的目的绝不仅是帮助个人按照自己的资历条件找到一份合适的工作，实现个人目标，更重要的是帮助个人真正了解自己，为自己设计出合理且可行的职业生涯发展方向。

典型问题

What are your career goals?
你的职业目标是什么？

相似问题

1. What goals do you have in your career?
在你的职业生涯中有什么目标？

2. What are your future plans?

你将来的计划是什么？

3. What are your long-term goals? What about in two and five years?

你的长期目标是什么？两年规划、五年规划分别是什么？

Words and Phrases	必备词汇
career [kəˈrɪə] *n.* 生涯；职业；事业	field [fiːld] *n.* 领域
planning [ˈplænɪŋ] *n.* 规划	spirit [ˈspɪrɪt] *n.* 精神
goal [gəʊl] *n.* 目标	advancement [ədˈvɑːnsm(ə)nt] *n.* 前进，进步；提升
short-term [ˌʃɔːtˈtɜːm] *adj.* 短期的	director [dɪˈrektə] *n.* 总监
ideal [aɪˈdɪəl; aɪˈdiːəl] *adj.* 理想的	shape [ʃeɪp] *n.* 形状 *vt.* 形成
constant [ˈkɒnst(ə)nt] *adj.* 经常的	strategic [strəˈtiːdʒɪk] *adj.* 战略上的
challenge [ˈtʃælɪndʒ] *n.* 挑战	intend to 打算做……，想要……
growth [grəʊθ] *n.* 增长；发展	hospitality [ˌhɒspɪˈtælɪti] *n.* 好客；服务业
professionally [prəˈfeʃənəli] *adv.* 专业地	talent [ˈtælənt] *n.* 才能；天才；天资
personally [ˈpɜːs(ə)n(ə)li] *adv.* 亲自地；就自己而言	vision [ˈvɪʒ(ə)n] *n.* 视力；美景；远见
expert [ˈekspɜːt] *adj.* 熟练的；*n.* 专家	ambition [æmˈbɪʃ(ə)n] *n.* 野心，抱负，志向
long-term [ˌlɒŋˈtɜːm] *adj.* 长期的	compliment [ˈkɒmplɪm(ə)nt] *n.* 恭维；称赞
technical [ˈteknɪkl] *adj.* 技术的	explain [ɪkˈspleɪn] *v.* 说明；解释
current [ˈkʌrənt] *adj.* 近期的，最近的	direction [dɪˈrekʃən] *n.* 方向
practical [ˈpræktɪkl] *adj.* 实际的，实用的	factor [ˈfæktə] *n.* 因素
multinational [ˌmʌltɪˈnæʃ(ə)n(ə)l] *adj.* 跨国公司的；多国的	priority [praɪˈɒrɪti] *n.* 优先；优先次序；优先考虑的事
gradually [ˈɡrædʒʊəli] *adv.* 逐步地	expertise [ˌekspɜːˈtiːz] *n.* 专门知识；专门技术
challenging [ˈtʃælɪndʒɪŋ] *adj.* 有挑战性的	local [ˈləʊk(ə)l] *adj.* 当地的
managerial [ˌmænəˈdʒɪːrɪəl] *adj.* 管理的	fulfill [fʊlˈfɪl] *vt.* 实现
possibility [ˌpɒsəˈbɪləti] *n.* 可能性	medium-term [ˈmiːdiəmˌtɜːm] *adj.* 中期的
transfer [trænsˈfɜː] to 转移到，调往	be competent [ˈkɒmpɪtənt] for 能胜任
regional [ˈriːdʒənl] *adj.* 地区的	grassroot *n.* 草根
oversee [ˌəʊvəˈsiː] *vt.* 监督；审查	green hand 新手
	elite [eɪˈliːt] *n.* 精英

Part 2　In an Interview 面试中

Mini Dialogues　迷你问答

Q: What is your ideal job?
A: My ideal job is one that gives me constant challenges and opportunities for growth both professionally and personally.
Q: What are your career goals?
A: I want to be an expert in my position.
Q: What is your long-term career goal?
A: My long-term goal is to move on from a technical position to a management position.
Q: What is your current goal if you work in our hotel?
A: I hope to develop my practical skills in a multinational hotel.
Q: If you could start your career again, what would you do differently?
A: Nothing. I am happy where I am today, so I don't want to change my past.

Q：你心目中的理想工作是什么？
A：我理想中的工作会让我常常遇到新的挑战，可以让我在专业能力和个人素质方面有成长的机会。
Q：你的职业目标是什么？
A：我想要成为行业的专家。
Q：你的长期职业目标是什么？
A：我的长期目标是从技术职位跃升到管理职位。
Q：如果你在我们酒店工作，你的近期目标是什么？
A：我希望能在一家跨国酒店提升自己的实践能力。
Q：如果可以重新开始你的职业生涯，你会有什么改变？
A：不会改变。我对现在的状况非常满意，所以不想改变过去。

Situational Dialogue 1　实战演习 1

A: What is your current goal if you work in our hotel?
B: I hope to grow gradually and gain more experience in your company in the coming years.
A: How long do you need to be an excellent employee?
B: I sincerely believe that I will become a very excellent employee in this field in three years with my spirit of study.
A: Why are you applying for this position?

A：如果你在我们酒店上班，你的近期目标是什么？
B：我希望在接下来的几年里能在贵公司逐渐成长，并获得更多的经验。
A：你需要多长时间成为一名出色的员工？
B：我坚信凭借我的学习精神，在3年之后我会成为这个领域的一名出色员工。
A：你为什么申请这个岗位？

酒店面试英语

续

Situational Dialogue 1

B: The reason why I am applying for this position is that this is a large company with a lot of opportunities for advancement. If I continue working in the department where this position is, I hope to be a director with a hand in shaping the strategic plans for development of the hotel.

A: Why do you choose our hotel?

B: I intend to work in the field of hospitality. That's why I want to work for ABC. As a leader in the industry, ABC has the resources, talent and the vision to be the best in the business. Working for this hotel is an ambition for many people in this field, and I'm no different.

A: Thank you for your compliment.

B: It's my pleasure.

实战演习 1

B：我应聘这个岗位的原因是这是一家大公司，大公司的提升机会会更多。如果我能够在该部门的该岗位持续工作，我希望可以成为部门总监，为酒店发展的战略规划献计献策。

A：你为什么选择来我们酒店工作？

B：我一直梦想去服务行业工作，这就是我为什么想选择 ABC 的原因。作为行业领军者，贵酒店有业内最佳资源、资质和发展远见。对于很多人而言，能为你们效劳可以说是远大的抱负，我也不例外。

A：感谢你的赞美之词。

B：我很荣幸。

Situational Dialogue 2

A: What's your long-term career goal?

B: I want to be an expert in my position.

A: That's good. Can you explain it?

B: The direction I would take in your hotel depends on many factors, such as the changing priorities of the market, the expertise I will have gained at the last five years, and the changing needs of your hotel.

A: That is challenging for you. Could you tell us about your plans in five years?

B: My goal is that in five years, I will be working in a managerial position in your hotel. I see the next few years here at ABC as an opportunity to gain skills and knowledge to run one of the departments. Another possibility in five years is to transfer to one of the regional offices, where I would oversee local operations. I will work hard to fulfill my dream.

实战演习 2

A：你的长期职业目标是什么？

B：我想要成为我所在职位的专家。

A：很好，你能解释一下吗？

B：我在贵酒店的职业发展方向取决于很多因素，比如市场重心的转变，近五年所学到的专业知识以及酒店需求的转变。

A：这对于你来说很有挑战性。分享一下你的五年计划吧？

B：我的目标就是在五年内可以在贵酒店获得一个管理岗位。如果能有幸进入 ABC 酒店工作，我一定抓住机会提升自身的专业技能，在未来的几年内成为一名部门领导。另外一种可能就是我可以被派到一个区域酒店，来负责其当地的业务。我会努力实现这一目标。

Part 2
In an Interview 面试中

练习

1. What is your short-term goal?
....
....
....
....

2. What is your long-term goal?
....
....
....
....

轻松一刻

A Present

Kate: Mom, do you know what I'm going to give you for your birthday?

Mom: No, honey. What?

Kate: A nice teapot.

Mom: But I've got a nice teapot.

Kate: No, you haven't. I've just dropped it.

Lesson 12　Hotels & Hospitality Industry
酒店和酒店业

章节说明

　　面试前，求职者应该对自己要去面试酒店的情况有一个基本的了解。例如，该酒店是否是国际连锁型酒店？该酒店隶属哪一家酒店集团？该酒店的市场定位、市场占有率、利润增长率、特色、企业文化如何？绝大多数酒店的相关信息可以在其网站上找到。面试前，求职者应仔细浏览，做到心中有数。回答问题时，要说明应聘酒店的优势及个人感兴趣的地方。

　　面试中，求职者应表现出对应聘酒店在该行业中的位置有相当的了解。如能表现出对酒店未来的发展方向有所了解则更好。

典型问题

What do you know about our hotel?
你对本酒店了解多少？

相似问题

1. What do you like about our hotel?
你喜欢本酒店的哪一点？

2. Why are you interested in our hotel?
你为什么对本酒店感兴趣？

3. What important trends do you see in our industry?
在我们所处的行业中，你看到了什么重要的趋势？

4. Do you know the history of our hotel group?
你了解我们酒店集团的历史吗？

5. What do you think about our hotel?
你认为我们酒店如何？

Words and Phrases 必备词汇

hospitality industry ['ɪndəstrɪ] 酒店业；服务业
trend [trend] n. 趋势，倾向；走向
be impressed [ɪm'prest] with 对……印象深刻
customer-centric ['sentrɪk] 以客户为中心的
commitment [kə'mɪtm(ə)nt] n. 承诺，保证
customer service 客户服务
extra ['ekstrə] n. 额外的事物；adj. 额外的
mile [maɪl] n. 英里；较大的距离
satisfied ['sætɪsfaɪd] adj. 感到满意的
Marriott ['mærɪət] 万豪酒店
competitive [kəm'petɪtɪv] adj. 竞争的；比赛的；求胜心切的
be eager to 盼望，渴望要做……
leading ['liːdɪŋ] adj. 领导的；主要的
daily ['deɪlɪ] adj. 日常的
arranged [ə'reɪndʒd] adj. 安排的
palace ['pælɪs] n. 宫殿
mainly ['meɪnlɪ] adv. 主要地，大体上

brand [brænd] n. 品牌
praise [preɪz] n. 赞扬；称赞
attract [ə'trækt] vt. 吸引
training courses 培训课程
firm [fɜːm] adj. 坚定的 n. 公司
rigorous ['rɪg(ə)rəs] adj. 严格的
reputation [repjʊ'teɪʃ(ə)n] n. 名声，名誉；声望
humanized ['hjuːmə,naizd] adj. 人性化的
fairly ['feəlɪ] adv. 相当地
Ritz-Carlton ['kɑːlt(ə)n] 丽思-卡尔顿酒店
super ['sjuːpə] adj. 特级的；极好的
luxury ['lʌkʃ(ə)rɪ] n. 豪华，奢侈；奢侈品
especially [ɪ'speʃ(ə)lɪ; e-] adv. 特别；尤其
motto ['mɒtəʊ] n. 座右铭
joint venture ['ventʃə] 合资企业
working language 工作语言
FBA (Food & Beverage Attendant) 餐饮服务生
banquet hall 宴会厅

Mini Dialogues	迷你问答
Q: What do you know about our hotel? A: I'm impressed with your hotel's customer-centric approach and commitment to providing excellent customer service. You go the extra mile to make sure your customers are satisfied. Q: Why are you interested in our hotel? A: Marriott is one of the most competitive hotel groups in the world. I've been eager to work for it for a long time. Q: What do you think about our hotel? A: Conrad is a leading hotel brand in the hospitality industry. Q: How much do you learn about our hotel? A: I have heard much praise for you. Q: Except the praise, are there still any other reasons that attract you to our hotel? A: InterContinental provide employees with excellent training courses. Q: What is the worst thing you have heard about our firm? A: How hard it is to get a job here and how tough and rigorous your interviews are.	Q：你对本酒店了解多少？ A：贵酒店秉承顾客至上的态度，致力于为顾客提供最优质的服务，令我印象深刻。为了让客人满意，你们尽心尽力。 Q：你为什么对本酒店感兴趣？ A：万豪是世界上最具竞争力的酒店集团之一，我渴望到贵酒店工作已经很长时间了。 Q：你认为我们酒店如何？ A：在酒店业，康莱德酒店是一流的酒店品牌。 Q：你对我们酒店了解多少？ A：我听过很多对贵酒店的好评。 Q：除了外界对酒店的好评之外，还有其他原因吸引你来我们酒店吗？ A：洲际酒店为员工提供优质的培训课程。 Q：你听到的与本酒店有关的最负面的事是什么？ A：（我听说）很难在贵公司谋得一职，面试特别严格。

Situational Dialogue 1	实战演习 1
A: Why do you choose our hotel? B: Your hotel enjoys a good reputation in the field. A: Could you share their praise with us? B: Your brand is on the top as to the hospitality industry. Moreover, your management is very humanized. A: Which point attracts you most? B: The opportunity you offer to your staff is fairly much.	A：你为什么选择我们酒店？ B：贵酒店在这个领域享有盛誉。 A：能和我们分享一下，人们是如何评价我们的吗？ B：贵酒店品牌在业界处于领先地位；此外，管理非常人性化。 A：哪一点最吸引你？ B：酒店提供给员工的机会很多。

Part 2

In an Interview 面试中

Situational Dialogue 2	实战演习 2
A: Do you know anything about our hotel? B: Yes, a little. The Ritz-Carlton is a super luxury brand of the Marriott hotel group. I especially like your motto—We are ladies and gentlemen serving ladies and gentlemen. A: Very good. What about your English? Ours is a joint venture. So, English is one of our working language. B: I can communicate with others in simple daily English. And I'm eager to learn more. A: Have you ever worked in a hotel? B: Yes. In fact, I often had my college-arranged short-term internships at Yuda Palace Hotel and J W Marriott Hotel in Zhengzhou. A: Really? Then what did you mainly do? B: Yes. I usually worked as a Food and Beverage Attendant at the banquet hall.	A：你了解我们酒店吗？ B：是的，了解一点。丽思卡尔顿是万豪酒店集团旗下的一个顶级奢华品牌。我特别喜欢贵酒店的座右铭：我们以绅士和淑女的态度为绅士和淑女忠诚服务。 A：很好。你的英语怎么样？我们是一家合资企业，所以英语是我们的工作语言之一。 B：我会用简单的日常英语和他人交流，并且，我非常渴望学习提高。 A：你曾经在酒店工作过吗？ B：是的。事实上，我经常参加学院安排的在郑州裕达国贸酒店或郑州绿地 J W 万豪酒店的短期实习。 A：是吗？你主要做什么工作？ B：是的。我通常是在酒店的宴会厅做餐饮服务生。

练习

What do you know about our hotel?

....
....
....
....

轻松一刻

That's Why

Jimmy started painting when he was three years old, and when he was five, he was already very good at it. He painted many beautiful and interesting pictures, and people paid a lot of money for them. They said, "This boy's going to be famous when he's a little older, and then we're going to sell these pictures for a lot more money."

Jimmy's pictures were different from other people's because he never painted on all of the paper. He painted on half of it, and the other half was always empty.

"That's very clever," everyone said. "Nobody else does that!"

One day somebody bought one of Jimmy's pictures and then said to him, "Please tell me this, Jimmy. Why do you paint on the bottom half of your pictures, but not on the top half?"

"Because I'm small," Jimmy said, "and my brushes don't reach very high."

Lesson 13　Working Attitude　工作态度

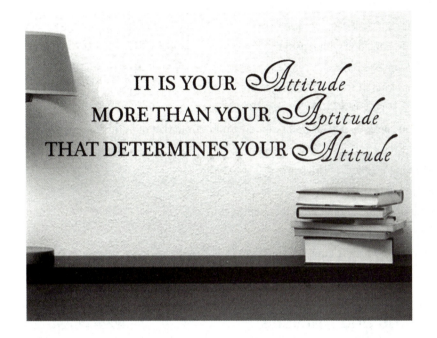

章节说明

当求职者的工作能力得到面试官的认可后，下一步他们将对求职者的工作态度进行考察。面试官不会直接问"你工作的态度怎么样？"这种具有明显倾向性的问题，而是会提出一些能反映出求职者工作态度的细节性问题。面对这种问题，求职者可以结合具体应聘的岗位来显示自身的敬业精神、责任心和对工作的热情，最好同时阐述能证明这些态度的过往经历，用事实赢得面试官的信任。

总之，在面试的时候，求职者要紧紧围绕所应聘的岗位的要求来回答问题，回答时要条理清楚，在表明观点后能用过往的实际经历来证实自身优点。对面试官要尊重但不惧怕，回答问题坦诚且客观。注意一些技巧，但关键还是自身的实力。

典型问题

How do you feel about working overtime?
你如何看待加班？

相似问题

1. Would you be able to work overtime if required?
必要的时候，你可以加班吗？
2. Would you be willing to relocate?
你愿意配合酒店调动工作地点吗？
3. How do you cope with tension?
你如何处理紧张的关系？
4. In what kind of work environment are you most comfortable?
你在什么样的工作环境下感觉最好？
5. Do you speak up if your point of view differs from that of your superior's?
如果你和上司意见不一致，你会提出来吗？
6. How do you handle criticism?
你如何对待批评？
7. What are some of the things that bother you?
什么事会使你困扰？
8. How do you handle stressful situations?
面对压力，你如何处理？

Words and Phrases	必备词汇
attitude ['ætɪtjuːd] *n.* 态度；看法 working overtime 加班 be willing to 愿意做…… relocate [ˌriː lə(ʊ)'keɪt] *v.* 重新分配 cope with 处理，对待 tension ['tenʃ(ə)n] *n.* 张力；紧张；不安 environment [ɪn'vaɪrənmənt] *n.* 环境 speak up 大声说出；毫无保留地说出 differ from 和……不同 superior [suː'pɪərɪə] *n.* 上司；高手；长者 handle ['hænd(ə)l] *v.* 处理，处置；对付 criticism ['krɪtɪsɪz(ə)m] *n.* 批评；考证；苛求 even if 即使 put off 推迟 relocation [ˌriːləʊ'keɪʃn] *n.* 重新分配 supportive [sə'pɔːtɪv] *adj.* 支持的 case [keɪs] *n.* 情况	bother ['bɒðə] *v.* 烦扰 stressful ['stresfl] *adj.* 有压力的 situation [ˌsɪtʃu'eɪʃn] *n.* 情形，情况 focus ['fəʊkəs] *n.* 焦点；中心 produce [prə'djuːs] *v.* 生产；引起；创造 extremely [ɪk'striːmlɪ; ek-] *adv.* 非常，极其 result-oriented ['ɔːrɪentɪd] *adj.* 以结果为导向的；注重结果的 invest [ɪn'vest] *v.* 投资；投入 task [tɑːsk] *vt.* 分派任务；*n.* 工作 complete [kəm'pliːt] *adj.* 完整的；完全的；彻底的；*vt.* 完成 hang out with sb. 和某人一起闲逛 express [ɪk'spres; ek-] *vt.* 表达 argue ['ɑːgjuː] with 争论；和……争吵 co-worker [ˌkəʊ'wɜːkə] *n.* 同事

Part 2
In an Interview 面试中

续

Words and Phrases | 必备词汇

establish *vt.* 建立
cordial ['kɔːdɪəl] *adj.* 热忱的，诚恳的
evidence ['evɪd(ə)ns] *n.* 证据
interpersonal skills 人际交往技能
function ['fʌŋ(k)ʃ(ə)n] *n.* 功能；*vi.* 运行；行使职责
positive ['pɒzɪtɪv] *adj.* 正面的
tidy ['taɪdɪ] *adj.* 整齐的
organized ['ɔːgəˌnaɪzd] *adj.* 有组织的；安排有秩序的；做事有条理的
essential [ɪ'senʃ(ə)l] *n.* 本质；要点；必需品；*adj.* 基本的，必要的
efficiency [ɪ'fɪʃ(ə)nsɪ] *n.* 效率；效能；功效
messy ['mesɪ] *adj.* 凌乱的，散乱的；肮脏的

miscommunication [ˌmɪskəˌmjuːnɪ'keɪʃən] *n.* 错误交流；交际失误
reasonable ['riːz(ə)nəb(ə)l] *adj.* 合理的，公道的；通情达理的
make a contribution [ˌkɒntrɪ'bjuːʃ(ə)n] to 对……做出贡献
present ['prezənt, prɪ'zent] *vt.* 提出；介绍；*adj.* 现在的；出席的；*n.* 现在；礼物
suggestion [sə'dʒestʃ(ə)n] *n.* 建议
disagreement [dɪsə'griːmənt] *n.* 不一致；争论；意见不同
complain about [kəm'pleɪn] 抱怨
pressure ['preʃə(r)] *n.* 压力
optimist ['ɒptɪmɪst] *n.* 乐观主义者；乐天派
self-regulation ['selfˌreɡjuː'leɪʃən] *n.* 自我调节

Mini Dialogues | 迷你问答

Q: How do you feel about working overtime?

A: My focus is not on the time I spend at work, but the results I'm expected to produce. I'm extremely result-oriented. I'm willing to invest whatever time it takes to produce the results.

Q: Would you be able to work overtime if required?

A: When I'm given a task to complete, I do so as soon as possible, even if that requires overtime. If there is something I could finish today, I'd rather finish it today than put it off until tomorrow.

Q: Would you be willing to relocate?

A: Certainly. For the relocation, I would get a chance to learn and grow both professionally and personally. My family is also very supportive of my career.

Q: 你如何看待加班？

A: 对我而言，重要的不是工作所花的时间，而是产生我所期望的结果。我是个非常重视结果的人，为了取得成果，我不在乎投入多少时间。

Q: 必要的时候，你可以加班吗？

A: 如果有工作要完成，即使加班，我也会尽早做完。今天能做完的事，我宁愿今天完成也不要拖到明天。

Q: 你愿意配合酒店调动工作地点吗？

A: 当然。我认为，改变工作地点不管对于工作还是个人，都是学习和成长的机会。我的家人也非常支持我的工作。

Mini Dialogues	迷你问答
Q: How do you cope with tension? A: In almost all cases, I was able to establish cordial relations with people around me. I think that is the strongest evidence of my interpersonal skills. Q: In what kind of work environment are you most comfortable? A: I function best in a positive but competitive environment. Q: How do you handle criticism? A: I think criticism provides a great opportunity to learn and grow. If I'm doing something wrong, I'd like to know so that I can correct and improve myself. Q: What are some of the things that bother you? A: I truly believe that a tidy, organized environment is essential to good performance and efficiency. I cannot stand a messy desk and office. Q: How do you handle stressful situations? A: I will hang out with my friends or just relax at home after finishing the work.	Q：你如何处理紧张关系？ A：在大多数情况下，我可以跟身边的人建立友好关系。我认为这也是我拥有较好的人际交往能力的一个强有力的证明。 Q：你在什么样的工作环境下感觉最好？ A：在积极又充满竞争的环境中，我最能发挥能力。 Q：你如何对待批评？ A：我认为别人的批评是一个让自己学习和成长的好机会。如果我某方面做错了，我想要知道，这样我才能改善和提高自己。 Q：什么事会使你困扰？ A：我深信，工作出成果、效率高需要整洁有序的环境。所以，我不能忍受桌子上和办公室里杂乱无章。 Q：面对压力，你如何处理？ A：完成工作后，我喜欢和朋友闲逛或者在家放松休息。

Situational Dialogue 1	实战演习 1
A: Do you speak up if your point of view differs from that of your superior's? B: I'm not a yes person, but I will be careful about how to express my opinions. A: What will you do then? B: I do not argue with the person, whether it's my superior or co-worker. A: Un-huh. B: Miscommunication is a common problem.	A：如果你和上司意见不一致，你会提出来吗？ B：我不是一个唯唯诺诺的人，但是我会注意表达自己观点时的措辞。 A：那你会怎么做呢？ B：我不会跟上司或者同事争论。 A：恩，是的。 B：误解是一个很普遍的问题。

Part 2 In an Interview 面试中

续

Situational Dialogue 1	实战演习 1
A: Right. B: So I want to make sure I understand their view correctly and how the person came to form that view. A: That's a reasonable way. B: And if I still believe my opinion can make a contribution, I present it as a suggestion, not as a disagreement or criticism. A: Very good.	A：是的。 B：所以，首先我会确认自己是否正确理解了对方的想法，是否了解对方为何会产生这样的想法。 A：这是一种比较理智的做法。 B：之后，如果仍然认为自己的意见能有所贡献，我会以建议的方式说明，而不是反对或批评别人的意见。 A：非常好。

Situational Dialogue 2	实战演习 2
A: Nowadays, more and more people begin to complain about the difficulty and pressure of their jobs. What about you? B: In my opinion, we always meet challenges in our work. And as for me, I enjoy it very much. A: You are such an optimist. B: Not really. Another reason is that I can work under pressure by self-regulation. A: How do you handle stressful situations? B: I share my stress with my friends. It really helps.	A：如今，越来越多的人开始抱怨工作上的困难和压力。你怎么看？ B：在我看来，我们在工作中总会遇到挑战。对我来说，我非常乐于接受挑战。 A：你真是一个乐天派。 B：也不完全是。还有一个原因是我能通过自我调节在压力下工作。 A：面对压力，你怎么处理？ B：我和朋友们分享我的压力。这真的很有用。

练习

1. How do you feel about working overtime?

....
....
....
....

2. How do you handle stressful situations?

....
....
....
....

轻松一刻

A Trip to Disney

On a trip to Disney World in Florida, my husband and I and our two children devoted ourselves wholeheartedly to the wonders of this attraction. After three exhausting days, we headed for home.

As we drove away, our son waved and said, "Good-by, Mickey."

Our daughter waved and said, "Good-by, Minnie."

My husband waved, rather weakly, and said, "Good-by, Money."

Lesson 14　Tough Questions
常见难题

章节说明

在面试中，求职者常常会遇到一些令人纠结的问题，例如："你最大的缺点是什么？""你曾经被解雇过吗？""我不确定你是否能够胜任这项工作。"回答稍有不慎，就会落入面试陷阱，从而落败。

求职者对待这类问题应该有一个积极正面的态度，牢记"推销"自己的初衷。

典型问题

What are some of your weaknesses?
你认为自己有哪些缺点？

相似问题

1. What is your greatest weakness?
你最大的缺点是什么？

2. What are your weak points?
你的短处是什么？

3. Do you think your lack of a degree/experience will affect your ability to perform the tasks required for the job?
你认为没有学位 / 工作经验会对你的工作造成影响吗？

4. Have you ever been fired?
你曾经被解雇过吗？

5. I'm not sure if you're suitable for the job.
我不确定你是否能够胜任这份工作。

6. Do you think we should hire you?
你认为我们应该雇用你吗？

7. What will you do if you don't get this position?
如果没有得到这个岗位，你会怎么做？

Words and Phrases	必备词汇
weakness ['wi:knəs] *n.* 弱点；软弱；嗜好 weak points 缺点；弱点 lack [læk] *n.* 缺乏；不足 *vt.* 缺乏；不足；没有；需要 *vi.* 缺乏；不足；没有 degree [dɪ'gri:] *n.* 程度，等级；度；学位 affect [ə'fekt] *vt.* 影响 perform [pə'fɔ:m] *vt.* 执行；完成；演奏 fire ['faɪə] *vt.* 解雇；点燃；激动 be suitable for 适合于……的 hire ['haɪə] *n&v.* 雇用 fair [feə] *adj.* 公平的；*adv.* 公平地；直接地；清楚地	share [ʃeə] *v.* 分享；*n.* 份额 stand [stænd] *vt.* 使站立；忍受；抵抗 recommend [rekə'mend] *v.* 推荐 exactly [ɪg'zæk(t)lɪ] *adv.* 恰好地；正是；精确地；正确地 pity ['pɪtɪ] *n.* 怜悯，同情；遗憾 respect [rɪ'spekt] *n&vt.* 尊敬，尊重 via ['vaɪə] *prep.* 渠道，通过；经由 regular ['regjʊlə] *adj.* 定期的；有规律的 be engaged in 参与；从事于；忙于 deal with 处理；处置；对付；应对 importance [ɪm'pɔ:t(ə)ns] *n.* 价值；重要

Part 2

In an Interview 面试中

Mini Dialogues | 迷你问答

Q: What are some of your weaknesses?

A: Sometimes I have a hard time saying no to people, and I end up taking on more than my fair share of the work.

Q: What is your greatest weakness?

A: I am sometimes a little bit ideal.

Q: Have you ever been fired?

A: Yes, it was my first part-time job because I didn't have any experience and was very nervous. Not only did I fail to serve the boss well, I also made a lot of frouble. A week later he couldn't stand me anymore and let me go.

Q: I'm not sure if you're suitable for the job.

A: May I ask why do you think so?

Q: Do you think we should hire you?

A: I highly recommend that.

Q: Are you applying for any other jobs?

A: Yes, but I'm most excited about this job because it is exactly what I want to do.

Q：你认为自己有哪些缺点？

A：有时候我不太会拒绝别人，所以做的事常常比别人多。

Q：你最大的缺点是什么？

A：我有时候有点理想化。

Q：你曾经被解雇过吗？

A：是的，那是我的第一份兼职工作，因为没有任何经验，所以我非常紧张。不但没能很好地为老板工作，还给他添了不少麻烦。一个星期后，他不愿再容忍，就解雇了我。

Q：我不确定你是否能够胜任这份工作。

A：您为什么会这么认为呢？

Q：你认为我们应该雇用你吗？

A：强烈推荐。

Q：你还在应聘其他工作吗？

A：是的，但是贵酒店的这份工作是我最感兴趣的。

Situational Dialogue 1 | 实战演习 1

A: What will you do if you don't get this position?

B: Sure I will feel it's a pity, but I will respect your decision.

A: If you don't get this job, what do you think would be the reasons?

B: I think it was something related to my working experience.

A: OK. I've no other questions. You will be informed of the interview results via E-mail by this Friday.

B: Thank you.

A：如果没有得到这个职位，你会怎么做？

B：我当然会感到惋惜，但我也会尊重你们的决定。

A：如果没得到这份工作，你觉得是什么原因呢？

B：我想可能和我的工作经验有关。

A：好的，我没有问题了。这周五前我们会通过电子邮件来告知你面试结果。

B：谢谢您。

酒店面试英语

Situational Dialogue 2	实战演习 2
A: It has been a year since you graduated and you are still out of work. B: Though I don't have a regular job, I am engaged in several part-time jobs during this time. A: What did you learn from these part-time jobs? B: I learned how to deal with people and I realized the importance of teamwork. A: What's your plan for the next step? B: Now I'm ready to start working.	A：毕业已经一年了，你还没有工作。 B：虽然我没有正式工作，但是这段时间我做了一些兼职工作。 A：从这些兼职工作中你学到了什么？ B：我学会了如何和人打交道，并且意识到了团队合作的重要性。 A：你接下来有什么打算？ B：现在我做好准备开始工作了。

练习

1. What are some of your weaknesses?
   ....
   ....
   ....
   ....

2. What will you do if you don't get this position?
   ....
   ....
   ....
   ....

轻松一刻

Charge for Bread and Butter

Some years ago, my dad, an attorney, took me to a fancy restaurant in New York city. When the bill arrived, there was a $1.50 charge for bread and butter. Dad paid the bill, including the charge for bread and butter. However, the next day, he sent a letter to the restaurant stating that the charge was uncalled for. Enclosed in the same envelope was a bill for $500 in legal services.

Someone from the restaurant called immediately and asked, "What is this $500 bill for? We never ordered any legal services."

Dad replied, "I never ordered any bread and butter."

The $1.50 was returned without delay.

Lesson 15 Asking Questions at Interview
向面试官提问

章节说明

在面试的最后阶段，面试官一般都会问"Do you have any questions?"或者"Is there anything you would like to say to close the interview?"之类的问题。对于上述问题，求职者千万不要马上回答"No"。因为如果不进行提问，很可能会被认为对所应聘的职位不感兴趣。

此时是求职者毛遂自荐的好时机。特别是你认为之前的面试进行得不太顺利时，可以借此机会，加强之前未能好好说明的事项，从而挽回局面。

面试者所提问题最好能围绕工作细节，这样会给面试官留下认真对待工作的好印象。

典型问题

What will my responsibilities be?
请问我的工作职责是什么？

相似问题

1. What training do you provide?
贵酒店提供什么样的培训？

Part 2
In an Interview 面试中

2. When will the training programs begin? What is the length of the training programs?
培训项目什么时候开始？培训时间有多久？

3. Is relocation likely now or in the future?
现在或未来有可能调动工作地点吗？

4. What qualities do you look for in new employees?
您希望新员工具备哪些素质？

5. How many employees does the department have?
请问这个部门有多少员工？

6. Is there anything I should be doing to prepare myself for the position?
在我入职之前，有哪些事是我应该做好准备的？

7. What do you like most about your job and the hotel?
您最喜欢您工作和酒店的哪些方面？

8. Why did you join the hotel?
您为何会进入这家酒店？

9. Could you tell me how your career has developed in this field?
可以告诉我您在酒店业的职业道路是怎么发展的吗？

Words and Phrases 必备词汇

Words and Phrases	必备词汇
responsibility [rɪˌspɒnsə'bɪlɪtɪ] *n.* 职责；责任	vacation [və'keɪʃn] *n.* 假期；度假
training program ['treɪnɪŋ 'prəʊɡræm] 培训项目	be supposed to 应该；被期望
length [leŋθ] *n.* 长度，长；时间的长短	intern ['ɪntɜːn] *n.* 实习生
quality ['kwɒlɪtɪ] *n.* 品质；才能	internship ['ɪntɜːnʃɪp] *n.* 实习；短期的实习
look for 寻找	qualify ['kwɒlɪfaɪ] *v.* 取得资格
prepare [prɪ'peə] for 准备；为……预备	spare [speə] *v.* 抽出（时间）
	promotion [prə'məʊʃn] *n.* 提升，晋升

Mini Dialogues 迷你问答

Mini Dialogues	迷你问答
Q: You may ask me any questions you have. A: OK. Thank you. Q: Can I ask you a question? A: Why not? Q: Is there anything else you'd like to know? A: No, not this time. Q: Do you have any questions you would like to ask me?	Q：你可以问任何问题。 A：好的，谢谢。 Q：我能问你一个问题吗？ A：当然可以。 Q：还有别的问题吗？ A：目前没有了。 Q：你有什么问题想问我吗？

Mini Dialogues	迷你问答
A: Would I have to work overtime very often?	A：我得常常加班吗？
Q: I've no further questions. Do you have any questions?	Q：我没有其他问题了。你有什么要问吗？
A: Yes, is there anything I should be doing to prepare myself for the position?	A：是的，在我入职之前，有哪些事是我应该做好准备的？
Q: Do you have any questions?	Q：你有什么问题要问吗？
A: When will the training programs begin? What is the length of the training programs?	A：培训项目什么时候开始？培训时间有多久？

Situational Dialogue 1	实战演习 1
A: Do you have any questions?	A：你有什么问题吗？
B: Yes. Do I have a vacation?	B：是的。我想知道是否有年假？
A: Generally, as for interns, you are supposed to work for 40 hours and enjoy two days off per week.	A：一般说来，作为实习生，你每周的工作时间是累计40小时，每周可以休息两天。
B: OK.	B：好的。
A: But you may have to work overtime sometimes.	A：但是有时也会需要加班。
B: No problem. I understand.	B：没问题，这个我理解。
A: After you've been here a year, you will qualify for a one-week vacation.	A：等你工作满一年，（转正后）你就有一周的年假。
B: That will be great.	B：那很好。
A: Anything else?	A：还有别的问题吗？
B: No, thanks.	B：没有了，谢谢。

Situational Dialogue 2	实战演习 2
A: Do you have any questions for us?	A：你有什么问题要问吗？
B: I was told you provide special language training program. I'm much interested in it.	B：我听说贵酒店提供专门的语言培训项目。我对此非常感兴趣。
A: Yes. Almost all employees in our hotel are supposed to spare one hour on average attending to the Russian training program.	A：是的。我们酒店几乎所有的员工平均每天要抽出一个小时的时间，参加公司的俄语培训。
B: A very good opportunity.	B：一个非常好的机会。

Part 2
In an Interview 面试中

续

Situational Dialogue 2	实战演习 2
A: You're right. B: Another question. Can I get a promotion during my internship? A: If you do the job well, you will. B: Thank you, Ma'am. I hope I will have the chance to work with you in the future. A: Thank you. B: Good-bye.	A：没错。 B：还有一个问题。实习期间，我有可能得到晋升吗？ A：如果你工作出色，会被晋升的。 B：谢谢您，女士。我希望将来能有机会和您一起工作。 A：谢谢。 B：再见。

练习

Do you have any questions for us?
....
....
....
....

轻松一刻

Hospitality

The hostess apologized to her unexpected guest for serving an apple-pie without any cheese. The little boy of the family left the room quietly for a moment and returned with a piece of cheese which he laid on the guest's plate.

The visitor smiled, put the cheese into his mouth and then said: "You must have better eyes than your mother, sonny. Where did you find the cheese?"

"In the rat-trap, sir," replied the boy.

Part 3

After an Interview

面试后

Lesson 16 Thank-you Letter 感谢信

章节说明

求职者撰写感谢信的目的是对面试官表达感谢,并表示对该工作相当有兴趣以及再次推荐自己。在信中还要强调自己的人格特质并表示未来会对酒店做出重要的贡献。在感谢信中应写明以下几点:①对面试官表示感谢;②能够见面谈话的喜悦;③希望加入酒店的意愿。在寄出邮件之前,应仔细检查遣词造句、拼写和标点符号是否正确,因为拼写和标点错误会留给他人不细心或不在乎的印象。

Checklist	备忘一览表
• A *different* thank-you note has been written for **each** person you met with individually. (Be sure to collect business cards during your interview to help you keep names and titles organized.)	• 感谢信应当写给每一位面试你的人。(面试时,请收集面试官们的名片,以确保正确称呼对方的名字和头衔。)
• All letters have been written and all will be mailed within **24 hours** of your interview.	• 所有的感谢信应当在面试后 24 小时内写好并寄出。

续

Checklist	备忘一览表
• In each thank-you letter you have followed up on specific things you talked about with the interviewer. You have mentioned something or someone that was particularly helpful, explain briefly why this job interested you and/or highlighted experiences or skills you failed to discuss in the interview. • You have reaffirmed your enthusiasm for the job opportunity and highlight your desire to take the next step and state briefly your suitability by touching on specific job-related strengths. • You have followed the rules for general job correspondence, including the use of professional language and a business like presentation. If you choose to hand a written thank-you letter, be sure that your handwriting is neat and legible. • Your letter is no longer than one page and is between 10 and 12 pt. font.	• 每一封感谢信应当紧密结合你和面试官在面试中谈到的一些具体问题。你可以提及对你有很大帮助的人或事，简要解释这份工作令你感兴趣的原因，强调指出你在面试时没有提到的经验或技能亮点。 • 你需要再次提到自己对这份工作机会的兴趣，强调希望有所进展，并通过和工作相关的优势来证明自己是合适的人选。 • 你要采用一般工作信件的要求，包括使用专业的语言和商业化的表述。如果是手写信函，请确保书写整洁、可辨识。 • 信件长度不要超过一页，字号在10磅到12磅之间。

Sentence Patterns	常用句型
Opening: • Thank you for taking the time... • I am writing to extend my sincere gratitude for... • I am writing to express my thanks for... • I am writing to show my sincere appreciation for... • I would like to convey in this letter my heartfelt thanks to you for... • I feel deeply indebted to you and I really don't know how to thank you enough for your help. • Thank you for seeing me on Wednesday regarding the Customer Service position.	引言： • 感谢您花时间…… • 我来信是为了……表达我真诚的谢意。 • 我写信的目的是感谢…… • 特别感激您…… • 真诚地想通过这封信来表示我……的万分感谢。 • 对于您的帮助，我感到万分感谢。 • 非常感谢您能够就我应聘客服人员一事，与我在星期三见面。

续

Sentence Patterns	**常用句型**
• Thank you for the opportunity to discuss your opening for a waiter. • Thank you for the time you took out of your busy schedule on Friday to discuss the requirements of the position of receptionist. • I want to thank you very much for interviewing yesterday for the position of baggage clerk. • I appreciated the opportunity to meet the staff of your department. **Central Section:** • The experience has confirmed my desire for employment with the ABC, Shanghai. • I was very impressed by your dynamic and rapidly growing hotel. • I was particularly impressed with ABC's strong commitment to innovation and growth. • The position is exciting because it seems to encompass a diversity of responsibilities. • I believe my experience in social practice, coupled with my studies in Hotel Management, will be an asset to your hotel. • My Hotel Management classes and part-time jobs have prepared me well for the position. • I would like to reiterate my interest in the position. • With my experience and skills, I would be able to contribute significantly to your hotel. • I sincerely feel that I am right for the job. • If I can provide any additional information, please call me at 135××××××××. • Please let me know if I can provide you with any additional information.	• 感谢您给我这次机会，就应聘餐饮服务员一职进行面谈。 • 感谢您能够在百忙之中抽出时间，就我应聘前台接待员一职与我在周五进行面谈。 • 非常感谢您昨天抽空对我应聘行李管理员一职进行面谈。 • 非常感谢能与贵部门的员工见面的机会。 **主体部分：** • 此次经历更加加深了我想在上海 ABC 酒店工作的意愿。 • 贵酒店充满活力，成长迅速，给我留下了深刻的印象。 • 我对 ABC 致力于改革和发展的坚定承诺印象特别深刻。 • 此职位的业务范围似乎非常广泛，让我感到很兴奋。 • 我相信我在大学期间所学的酒店管理知识和从社会实践中获得的经验，将对贵酒店有所贡献。 • 我所拥有的酒店管理知识和兼职工作经验，为我胜任此职位做好了充分准备。 • 我想再次表达我对此职位深感兴趣。 • 我相信凭借自己的经验与技能，一定会对贵酒店有很大的贡献。 • 我真诚地认为自己是这个职位的不二人选。 • 如果需要我提供其他资料，请拨打 135×××××××× 通知我。 • 如果需要我提供其他资料，请通知我。

酒店面试英语

Sentence Patterns	常用句型
• I look forward to joining your management team. **Close:** • Thank you again for the time and courtesies you and your associates extended to me. I must thank you again for your generous help. • I am most grateful for your interview. • My true gratitude is beyond the words' description. • I feel most obliged to thank you once more. • Please accept my gratitude, now and always.	• 我期待能够加入贵酒店的管理团队。 结语： • 再次感谢您和您的同事能抽空与我见面并且多方照顾。我必须对您的慷慨帮助再次致谢。 • 参加这次面试我特别感激。 • 我的感谢之情无以言表。 • 再次感谢您。 • 请接受我的感激之情。

Model 1　Thank-you Letter (Br. E) 英式感谢信

写信人地址置于信的右上角	Sophie Suo No. 1 Yuying Rd. Guangcheng District Zhengzhou 450000 Telephone: 135××××××××
	15 May, 2018
其他细节信息按照完全平头式从页面左边空白处写起	Mr. Wang HR Director ABC Hotel Shanghai No. 6 Nanjing Rd. Shanghai 201800 Dear Mr. Wang,
感谢面试机会	It was a pleasure meeting with you yesterday. I appreciated the opportunity to talk with you in person about the position of Food & Beverage Attendant.

续

Model 1 Thank-you Letter (Br. E) 英式感谢信

对工作的热情，突出自己的优势	Our meeting confirmed my interest in the position and enthusiasm for working for ABC, Shanghai. I believe that my education, techniques in F&B services and interpersonal skills will enable me to fulfill the challenges of the position and contribute significantly to your hotel. I am excited about the chance to work in such a challenging environment.
再次感谢	Thank you again for the opportunity to learn more about your hotel. As you suggested, I will call you next week to check the status of the hiring process. In the meantime, if I can provide you with more information, please let me know. I can be reached at 135×××××××× or 135×××××××@139.com. I hope to be hearing from you soon. Yours truly, Sophie Suo

Model 2 Thank-you Letter (Am. E) 美式感谢信

写信人地址置于信的左上角	Adam Wang No. 188 Jinlong Rd. Zhengzhou 450000 May 24, 2016
其他细节信息按照完全平头式从页面左边空白处写起	Ms. Dorothy Li HR Director ABC Hotel No. 9 Xueyuan Rd. Haidian District Beijing 100080 Dear Ms. Li, Thank you very much for taking time out of your busy schedule to meet with me about the Housekeeping Attendant position this morning. I enjoyed meeting with you and learning more about the position and ABC Hotel. The position is exactly what I am looking for.

续

Model 2　Thank-you Letter (Am. E) 美式感谢信

	I am confident that my major of Hotel Management fit nicely with the job requirements and I could make significant contribution to the hotel. I would welcome the opportunity to work for ABC Hotel. I would like to meet with you again to further discuss this position and my qualifications. I will be happy to provide any other information you may need to assist in your decision. Thank you again for your time and consideration. I look forward to hearing from you very soon and hope I will have the opportunity to work with you. Sincerely, Adam Wang

Model 3　Thank-you Letter (E-mail) 电子邮件感谢信

打开收件箱的页面	**Inbox**
信件的主题（Subject）	**Thank you for your interview**
	From: Frank Zhang <1234567@qq.com>
	Date: Wednesday, May 18, 2016 5:10 PM
	To: Ricky Li < ricky.li@hg.com >
	Cc: Grace Zhang <grace.zhang@hg.com>; Christine Hu <christine.hu@hg.com >
	File : 1 Attachment (Resume-Frank Zhang. docx)
正式的称呼	Dear Human Resources Director Mr. Ricky Li,
句子简洁	Thank you for interviewing me for the Concierge position today. The tour of your hotel and conversations with your staff gave me a clearer view of the duties of the position and increased my interest.
段落简短。 段落之间空一行	The position seems quite challenging and I am very enthusiastic about joining your first-class team. I believe that my work experience and my educational background in Hotel Management qualify me for the position.

Part 3 After an Interview 面试后

续

Model 3 Thank-you Letter (E-mail) 电子邮件感谢信

标准的"署名"模块	If you have any other questions, please contact me at 135×××××××× anytime. If I do not hear from you by next week, I will call you to see how your selection process is processing. I look forward to hearing from you. Yours truly Frank Zhang 张诚 Hotel Management Major 酒店管理专业 Zhengzhou Tourism College 郑州旅游职业学院 1234567@qq.com |Tel: 135××××××××
	Compose
	To:
	Add Cc
	Subject:
	Attach files
	Content

Model 4 Thank-you Letter (Letterhead Format) 信头式感谢信

写信人地址置于信的中间模仿信封的写法	**Francis Bush** CMR 9999 St. Lawrence University Canton, NY 13617 August 15, 2015 Mr. Jack Brown Human Resources Manager Brown Consulting 5588 Main Street Chicago, IL 99988

Model 4 Thank-you Letter (Letterhead Format) 信头式
感谢信

Dear Mr. Brown,

It was a pleasure to meet with you and your staff on Monday, August 14. I was very impressed with your organization and am extremely interested in the consultant position at Brown Consulting. I want to take this opportunity to thank you for arranging such an informative and productive visit during which I was able to see the firm and meet with many of your colleagues.

The consultant position at Brown is both exciting and challenging, and I am confident that my background and qualifications would enable me to contribute effectively to the consulting team. Through my internship experience at Greenwood Consulting, and my work with the economics department at St. Lawrence University, I developed strong communication and leadership skills in both academic and corporate environments.

Once again, thank you for taking the time to arrange my visit. If there is any additional information required supporting my candidacy, please do not hesitate to contact me. Thank you for your time, attention and consideration. I look forward to hearing from you soon.

Kind regards,
Francis Bush
Francis Bush

Summary	小结
• Correct names, titles and contact details • Within 24 hours of the job interview • Be short and to the point • Legible handwriting • Spell check and proof-read	• 正确的称呼及细节 • 面试后 24 小时内写好、寄出 • 要简短、切题 • 适当时可手写，易于辨认 • 检查拼写，进行相关校对

练习

Write a short thank-you letter. Include your reasons why you are suitable for the job and express your thankfulness.

职场解密

Guidelines for Interview

- Prepare to introduce yourself immediately during the interview.
- The campus presentation by different hotels is to be used for information gathering. DO NOT ask for a job or internship. If they feel they can offer something else, let them initiate these ideas.
- Discuss your background, skills and career interests. Let the interviewers know what you have done in your college life, what activities you are involved in on campus, and emphasize your key leadership experiences.
- Never assume interviewers will contact you. Generally, interviewees should phone the interviewers to make arrangements for an informational interview, conversation or meeting.
- In your letter/text/WeChat, mention the mode of follow-up you are going to use (phone, E-mail, etc.) and then make it your responsibility to do so within 2 weeks before the final interview.
- Be prepared to make several attempts to contact the interviewer before you connect; these individuals are busy professionals who have many commitments to juggle. Don't be discouraged if you experience a delay.
- If you make an appointment, be there, be on time, and dress appropriately.
- Always write a thank-you letter in response to help that you have received from the interviewer.

Remember that website is just one way to gather career-related information. Contact parents, friends, faculty, past employers, community members and other individuals working in areas that you're interested in for additional information and for possible interview opportunities.

Appendix 1 Hotel Groups
酒店集团

1. Marriott International, Inc.（万豪国际酒店集团）

Marriott

Marriott International, Inc. (NASDAQ: MAR) is an American multinational diversified hospitality company that manages and franchises a broad portfolio of hotels and related lodging facilities. Founded by J. Willard Marriott, the company is now led by his son, Executive Chairman Bill Marriott and President and Chief Executive Officer Arne Sorenson.

Marriott International, headquartered in Bethesda, Maryland in the Washington, DC metropolitan area, has more than 4,087 properties in over 80 countries and territories around the world, over 697,000 rooms (as of July 2014), and additional 195,000 rooms in the development pipeline.

In June 2014, Marriott International opened their 4,000th hotel, the Marriott Marquis in Washington, D.C. On November 16, 2015, Marriott International announced it would purchase Starwood Hotels and Resorts Worldwide for $13.6 billion, presumably creating the world's largest hotel chain once a closed deal.

Operations

Marriott is the first hotel chain to serve food that is completely free of trans fats at all of its North American properties.

The hotel is noted for including copies of the Book of Mormon in addition to the Holy Bible in its rooms.

Brands

Marriott operates 30Brands internationally.

Signature brand
- Marriott Hotels & Resorts（万豪）
- Delta Hotels

Luxury
- BVLGARI Hotels & Resorts（宝格丽）
- JW Marriott Hotels & Resorts（JW 万豪）
- Ritz-Carlton（丽思卡尔顿）

Lifestyle/collections
- AC Hotels by Marriott
- Autograph Collection Hotels（傲途格精选酒店）

- EDITION Hotels（艾迪逊）
- Renaissance Hotels（万丽）
- MOXY Hotels

Destination entertainment
- Gaylord Hotels
- Marriott Vacation Club (MVC)（万豪度假俱乐部）

Select-service lodging
- Courtyard by Marriott（万怡）
- Fairfield Inn by Marriott（万豪费尔菲德）
- Protea Hotels by Marriott（普罗蒂）
- SpringHill Suites by Marriott（万豪春丘）

Extended-stay lodging
- Residence Inn by Marriott（万豪居家）
- TownePlace Suites by Marriott（万豪汤普雷斯）
- Marriott Executive Apartments

Timeshare
- Marriott Grand Residence Club
- The Residences at the Ritz-Carlton
- The Ritz-Carlton Destination Club

Conference centers
- Marriott Conference Centers

Great America Parks

Marriott also developed three and ultimately opened two theme parks entitled Marriott's Great America from 1976 until 1984. The parks were located in Gurnee, Illinois; Santa Clara, California; and a proposed but never-built location in the Washington, DC area, and were themed celebrating American history.

The following list of former Starwood brands is chronological, according to each brand's entry into Starwood:

Westin（威斯汀）

The Westin Hotels and Resorts brand is Starwood's largest upscale hotels and resorts brand. It was bought by Starwood in 1994 and is also the oldest brand within Starwood, dating back to 1930 and still continuing with it.

Sheraton（喜来登）

Sheraton is Starwood's "flagship" brand, providing luxury hotel and resort accommodation. It began operating in 1937 and was sold to Starwood in 1998 by ITT. Also under the Sheraton brand are 7 Vacation Ownership properties.

The Luxury Collection（豪华精选）

The Luxury Collection brand began in 1994 when ITT Sheraton purchased a controlling interest in CIGA (Compagnia Italiana Grandi Alberghi, or Italian Grand Hotels Company), a super elite Italian based international hotel chain which owned a significant number of the world's most famous and exclusive hotels. Those hotels, as well as a number of top-tier Sheraton Hotels, were then marketed as ITT Sheraton Luxury Hotels. After Starwood bought Sheraton, they established a separate brand identity for The Luxury Collection and expanded it.

Both ITT Sheraton and later Starwood kept CIGA's original logo (the four horses of St. Mark) for The Luxury Collection brand logo until 2010; each Luxury Collection hotel now uses its own logo. Many hotels in The Luxury Collection are smaller establishments in converted palaces or other significant buildings, others are restored historic hotels.

Confusingly, some hotels in The Luxury Collection which were originally part of the ITT Sheraton Luxury group kept their Sheraton name when the Luxury division was spun off as a completely separate brand under Starwood. There are four such hotels remaining today, operating with the name Sheraton, but not technically part of Sheraton. These hotels are the Sheraton Addis (Addis Ababa, Ethiopia), Sheraton Grande Sukhumvit (Bangkok, Thailand), Sheraton Algarve Hotel (Albufeira, Portugal), and Sheraton Kuwait Hotel (Kuwait City, Kuwait).

A part of the Collection, the Royal Penthouse Suite, at Hotel President Wilson in Geneva, billed at US$65,000 per night, is listed at number 1 on World's 15 Most Expensive Hotel Suites list compiled by CNN Go in 2012.

Four Points by Sheraton (福朋)

Launched in 1995 under the Sheraton Group's brand, this brand is a set of mid-range hotels that replaced the Sheraton Inn sub-brand of Sheraton.

W Hotels (W 酒店)

W Hotels is Starwood's luxury boutique hotel brand, generally marketed towards a younger crowd. It was launched in 1998 with the W New York, a conversion of the old Doral Inn hotel at 541 Lexington Avenue in Manhattan and the brand has since expanded with over fifty hotels and resorts around the world.

Though the hotels vary from newly built flagship properties to more modest conversions of previous hotels, they have a common theme of spare, minimalist modern decor and hip, informal names for categories of rooms and public areas. For example, the lobbies of all the hotels are known as the "Living Room". W Hotels attempt to include the letter W wherever possible- the swimming pool is known as "Wet", the concierge is known as "Whatever Whenever", the laundry bag in every room is known as "Wash", and so on.

St. Regis (瑞吉)

St. Regis is Starwood's main luxury brand, launched in 1999. It is named for The St. Regis Hotel in New York, which was built in 1904 in Manhattan at 5th Avenue and 55th Street by John Jacob Astor IV, who also founded the Astoria Hotel (which later became the Waldorf-Astoria Hotel) and who died in 1912 on the RMS Titanic. In the 1930s, head bartender Fernand Petiot, introduced the Bloody Mary cocktail. The St. Regis was a Sheraton from 1966 on, and following a lavish restoration from 1985 to 1991 was part of the ITT Sheraton Luxury division before it became the cornerstone and flagship of Starwood's new brand. The brand is currently present on four continents with a total pipeline of 57 operating and signed hotels as of April 2016.

Le Méridien (艾美)

Le Méridien was founded by Air France in 1972 and was sold to Starwood in 2005, by which point it was based in the UK. It has a total of 137 properties operating or in the pipeline worldwide, with its first property being Le Méridien Etoile in Paris, France. Le Méridien is positioned as an upper-upscale brand in the Starwood hierarchy and offers properties with an edge towards art, design and local destination, with each hotel customized to its respective location with the intent of "unlocking destinations" for guests. Certain locations offer guests complimentary access to art galleries and museums through collaborations and partnerships. Le Méridien has a partnership with the Italian coffee roasting company Illy, serving and promoting Illy-branded coffee and products throughout its hotels around the world.

Aloft, a Vision of W Hotels (雅乐轩)

Aloft is a mid-scale, urban-style business / boutique hotel brand. The brand was launched in 2005, in a relationship with W similar to Four Points by Sheraton and its "brand parent", Sheraton.

Element by Westin (源宿)

Announced in 2006, this is Starwood's first brand of hotels intended to be environmentally friendly. The designs include energy and water efficient features. The first Element hotel opened in Lexington, Massachusetts in July 2008. Element hotels are built eco-friendly from the ground up, from the floors made of recycled materials to energy-efficient lighting and plumbing fixtures. In 2013 the first Canadian location opened in Vaughan, Ontario. In September 2014 the first German location opened in Frankfurt.

Tribute Portfolio (臻品之选)

Launched in April 2015, Tribute Portfolio is the 10th brand of Starwood. Similar to The Luxury Collection brand, Tribute Portfolio is a collection of independent hotels but with a focus on four-star hotels instead of five-star ones. Individual hotels under this brand gain access to Starwood's sales platform and participate in the Starwood Preferred Guest loyalty program but do not share their look and feel.

Design Hotels

Berlin-based Design Hotels provides hospitality services to a network of nearly 300 independently owned and operated hotels. Starwood has been a majority investor in the Design Hotels since 2011. In October 2015, Starwood announced that it would add Design Hotels to its brand portfolio through a new marketing partnership. Member hotels of the Design Hotels collection have the option to join the Starwood Preferred Guest loyalty program and gain access to Starwood's sales platform. Design Hotels continues to operate independently.

Advertisement

  Thinking of you! 全心为你！ (Marriott)
  Collect the world's experience! 精选世界的风采！ (The luxury Collection)
  Explore & Experience. 探索，体验！ (Westin)
  Well. Hello there. W 酒店，欢迎您！ (W Hotels)

2. Hilton Worldwide Holdings, Inc.（希尔顿全球控股有限公司）

  Hilton Worldwide Holdings, Inc. (formerly, Hilton Worldwide and Hilton Hotels Corporation) is an American multinational hospitality company that manages and franchises a broad portfolio of hotels and resorts. Founded by Conrad Hilton in 1919, the corporation is now led by Christopher J. Nassetta.

  Hilton Worldwide is headquartered in Tysons Corner, Virginia. As of June 30 2016, its portfolio includes 4,726 properties with 775,866 rooms in 104 countries & territories, making the corporation the largest hotel chain in the world by rooms and international presence. Prior to their December 2013 IPO, Hilton was ranked as the 36th largest privately held company in the United States by *Forbes*.

  Hilton Worldwide has 13 brands across different market segments including Conrad Hotels & Resorts, Canopy by Hilton, Curio—A Collection by Hilton, Hilton Hotels & Resorts, DoubleTree by Hilton, Embassy Suites Hotels, Hilton Garden Inn, Hampton Inn（汉普顿旅馆）, Homewood Suites by Hilton, Home2 Suites by Hilton, Hilton Grand Vacations and Waldorf Astoria Hotels & Resorts. In January 2016 Hilton unveiled its new midscale-market brand, Tru by Hilton.

  On December 12, 2013, Hilton again became a public company in its second IPO to raise an estimated $2.35 billion. The Blackstone Group holds a 45.8% stake in the company.

  Conrad Hilton founded the company in Cisco, Texas in 1919 and established headquarters in Beverly Hills, California from 1969 until 2009. The company moved to Tysons Corner, unincorporated Fairfax County, Virginia, near McLean in August 2009.

Brands

  Luxury
- Conrad Hotels & Resorts（康莱德）
- Waldorf Astoria Hotels and Resorts（华尔道夫）

  Full service
- Hilton Hotels & Resorts（希尔顿）
- DoubleTree by Hilton（希尔顿逸林）

- Embassy Suites by Hilton（大使套房酒店）
- Curio, A Collection by Hilton

Focused service
- Hilton Garden Inn（花园酒店）
- Hampton by Hilton（欢朋）
- Homewood Suites by Hilton（家木套房酒店）
- Home2 Suites by Hilton
- Tru by Hilton

Lifestyle
- Canopy by Hilton

Timeshare
- Hilton Grand Vacations（希尔顿度假俱乐部）

Defunct
- Denizen Hotels (Defunct)
- Lady Hilton (Defunct)

Franchising

As of 2013, about 70% of the rooms branded under Hilton Worldwide were franchised to independent operators and companies. During its 2007—2013 ownership of Hilton Worldwide, Blackstone Group pursued a strategy of predominantly expanding Hilton's reach through franchise agreements, while relatively few new properties were actually operated by Hilton. Hence, the proportion of franchised rooms grew significantly during this period. The practice of franchising is popular within the hospitality industry among most major hotel chains, as the parent company does not have to pay for the maintenance and overhead costs of franchised properties. Franchisees must follow strict brand standards in order to maintain a licensing agreement with Hilton Worldwide. Most of Hilton's flagship properties, airport properties and largest resorts, however, are corporately managed.

Company culture

According to Careerbliss.com, Hilton Worldwide ranked first in the "2012 Happiest Companies in America", with a score of 4.36 out of 5. The survey looked at job reviews from more than 100,000 employees such as characteristics like work-life balance, company culture and reputation, and the relationships employees have with their bosses. Additionally, Hilton has scored 100% on the Corporate Equality Index for the past nine years.

Advertisememnt

Travel is more than just A to B. 旅行不仅是 A 地到 B 地。（Hilton）

The luxury of being yourself. 做高贵的你！（Conrad）

This summer is packed with the fun of kids at doubletree! 今年夏天双树酒店充满了孩子们的欢乐！(Doubletree)

3. InterContinental Hotels Group (洲际酒店集团)

InterContinental Hotels Group PLC informally InterContinental Hotels or IHG is a British multinational hotels company headquartered in Denham, UK. IHG has over 742,000 rooms and 5,028 hotels across nearly 100 countries. Its brands include Candlewood Suites, Crowne Plaza, Even, Holiday Inn, Holiday Inn Express, Hotel Indigo, Hualuxe, InterContinental and Staybridge Suites. Of the 4,602 hotels, 3,934 operate under franchise agreements, 658 are managed by the company but separately owned, and 10 are directly owned.

Bass Hotels

The origins of InterContinental Hotels Group can be traced back to 1777, when William Bass established the Bass Brewery in Burton-upon-Trent. In 1876, its red triangle trademark was the first registered in the United Kingdom.

In 1989, the British Government limited the number of pubs which brewers could directly own, resulting in Bass investing in the expansion of its small line of hotels. In 1990, it purchased Holiday Inn International from Kemmons Wilson and expanded into North America.

Operations

The company worldwide headquarters and Europe offices are in Denham, Buckinghamshire in England. The Americas office is in Dunwoody, Georgia in Greater Atlanta. The Asia, Middle East and Africa offices are in Singapore. The Greater China offices are in Pudong, Shanghai.

In 2006, IHG and Lend Lease Group (Lend Lease US Public Partnerships), joined forces in the Privatization of Army Lodging program. IHG Army Hotels is a division of IHG that manages on-post hotels and lodgings in 39 different locations in the U.S., including Puerto Rico.

Brands

- Candlewood Suites（烛木套房酒店）
- Crowne Plaza（皇冠假日酒店）
- Holiday Inn Hotels & Resorts, the number two hotel brand in the world by number of rooms（假日酒店）
- Holiday Inn Club Vacations
- Holiday Inn Express (formerly known as Express by Holiday Inn in Europe, Middle East, Africa, Asia Pacific and South America)（智选假日酒店）
- Hotel Indigo（英迪格酒店）

- InterContinental（洲际酒店及度假村）
- Staybridge Suites（斯桥套房酒店）

In February 2012, IHG announced plans for a new wellbeing based concept called Even Hotels and in March 2012, a new luxury concept called "Hualuxe" to be rolled out initially in China.

16 December 2014, IHG announced it would acquire Kimpton Hotels & Restaurants for $430 million in cash. IHG plans to retain the Kimpton brand within the U.S. and expand it globally. The combined IHG-Kimpton portfolio will create the world's largest boutique hotel business.

Advertisement

We know what it takes. 明白所需，满足所想。（Intercontinental）

Be yourself. 自在自我。（Holiday Inn）

4. Wyndham Hotels & Resorts（温德姆酒店集团）

Wyndham Hotels & Resorts is a hotel and resort chain based in the United States. It has locations in Canada, Mexico, Colombia, Ecuador, Turkey, Germany, the UK and the Caribbean. The company sold many of its hotels in the early 2000s.

History

Wyndham Hotel Corporation was founded in 1981 in Dallas, Texas, by Trammell Crow, the president of Trammel Crow Company (TCC). The company appears to have been named after a friend of Crow's, a woman named Wyndham Robertson, who wrote a profile of him for *Fortune* magazine. As the company grew, it eventually merged with a hotel REIT called Patriot American Hospitality (PAH). Patriot American organized the combined company as a paired-share REIT, in which Patriot owned the real estate assets and leased the hotels to Wyndham to run.

The firm grew rapidly in the late 1990s, acquiring multiple portfolios of hotels and renaming them Wyndhams. In 1998, in an effort to build an upscale limited-service brand, the company acquired the Summerfield Hotel Corporation and renamed it **Summerfield Suites by Wyndham.** Wyndham Garden Hotels are smaller properties, usually full-service, that are located in suburban or airport locations. Later that year, the combined company introduced a short-lived luxury brand, **Grand Bay Hotels & Resorts**, which would include 11 hotels that the company had acquired over the past few years and would turn Patriot into a multi-brand hotel operating and ownership organization. The company also included several European properties, including **The Great Eastern Hotel** in the City of London.

However, the company's rapid growth drained cash and the firm was unable to continue to grow on its own. In March, 1999, the group agreed to a $1 billion restructuring when a consortium of private equity firms, including Thomas H. Lee Partners and Apollo Real Estate Advisors, assumed control of the company. They renamed it **Wyndham International**. The company's paired share status was dropped, and Wyndham International re-emerged as a C corporation.

From 1999 to 2004, the firm struggled to pay down debt and was forced to sell off many of the hotels it had acquired in the late 1990s, often at a deep discount in an industry still suffering from the effects of the 9/11 terrorist attacks. The effort to expand the **Grand Bay Hotels & Resorts** brand was canceled, and the brand's franchised limited-service offerings, **Summerfield Suites** and Wyndham Garden Hotels, continued to lose units as hotels converted out of the system. Many of the Summerfield Suites hotels were sold to the Intercontinental Hotels Group and were converted to Staybridge Suites hotels.

In June, 2005, Wyndham International was acquired by affiliates of the Blackstone Group, for $3.24 billion and taken private. In the subsequent months, many of its hotels were sold to Goldman Sachs Group and Columbia Sussex. Blackstone rebranded most of the remaining assets as **LXR Luxury Resorts** and sold the Wyndham and Wyndham Garden Hotel brands to Cendant. Blackstone sold Summerfield Suites to Hyatt Hotels, which renamed it Hyatt House.

On August 1, 2006, all Cendant hotel brands became part of Wyndham Worldwide. Wyndham Worldwide consists of the following brands of hotels: Baymont Inn & Suites, Days Inn, Howard Johnson's, Knights Inn, Microtel, Ramada, Super 8, Travelodge, Wyndham, Wyndham Garden Hotels, Hawthorn Suites and Wingate by Wyndham. Besides hotels, the company also operates Wyndham Vacation Resorts (formerly Fairfield Resorts) and WorldMark by Wyndham (formerly Trendwest) time share resorts.

In 2013, Wyndham Worldwide acquired Shell Vacations Club for $102 million including $153 million of debt.

The Federal Trade Commission (FTC) filed suit against Wyndham in June 2012 following a security breach that led to the theft of payment card data for hundreds of thousands of Wyndham customers. Wyndham decided to fight the lawsuit in court, unlike many companies, which often try to settle FTC data-security enforcement actions quickly. In April 2014, United States District Court for the District of New Jersey Judge Esther Salas denied Wyndham's motion to dismiss, in a much-anticipated decision to this case.

Advertisement

Leave the rest to us. 将余下的交给我们。(Ramada)

The best value under the sun. 天下最划算的地方。(Days Inn)

5. Jinjiang International [上海锦江国际酒店（集团）股份有限公司]

Jinjiang International (Group) Company Limited is a Shanghai-based state-owned enterprise of the People's Republic of China and one of the largest tourism enterprises in China.

Its subsidiaries include Jin Jiang International Holdings Limited, Jin Jiang International Hotel Management Company Limited and Jin Jiang Inn Company Limited.

The Group operates Shanghai's well known Jinjiang Hotel, Peace Hotel, Park Hotel and Metropole Hotel. Other chains operated by the group include the Jinjiang Inn (锦江之星), Bestay Hotel Express (百时快捷酒店) and Magnotel (白玉兰酒店).

Subsidiary enterprises

Jinjiang Hotels

Shanghai Jinjiang International Hotels Holdings Company Limited (Jinjiang Hotels Group or Jinjiang Hotels in short form) is the largest hotel group in China. It has more than 380 hotels and inns affiliated to it and under its management in major China cities, including Peace Hotel and Jinjiang Star.

The Group's subsidiary company, Shanghai Jinjiang International Hotel Development Company Limited (SSE: 600754) was listed on the Shanghai Stock Exchange in 1996. Its holding company, Shanghai Jinjiang International Hotels (Group) Company Limited H shares (SEHK: 2006) was listed on the Hong Kong Stock Exchange in 2006.

Jin Jiang International Hotel Management Company Ltd. (锦江国际酒店管理有限公司) has its headquarters in Pudong, Shanghai.

6. AccorHotels (雅高酒店集团)

AccorHotels, formerly known as Accor S.A., is a French multinational hotel group, part of the CAC 40 index, which operates in 94 countries and regions.

Headquartered in Paris, France, the group owns, operates and franchises 3,700 hotels on five continents representing several brands, from budget and economy lodgings to five-star hotels.

Economy brands

In August 2012, Accor announced its economy brands would be converted into "the ibis family", including three complementary brands—ibis (宜必思), ibis budget (formerly Etap Hotel) and ibis Styles (formerly All Seasons). All ibis Family brands feature the SweetBed. In 2014, the brand launched its new restaurant concept: ibis Kitchen.

hotel F1 is a chain of 238 "no frills" budget hotels in France. Guestrooms are equipped with a wash corner and each floor offers shared bathroom and shower facilities.

ibis budget (*blue logo*) has 541 hotels in 17 countries and regions. The full network uses the brand's "cocoon concept", awarded Best Interior Design at the 2008 European Design Awards. In 2012 ibis budget was created from the re-branding of former Etap Hotels and Formule 1 hotels.

ibis Styles (*green logo*) has 293 hotels in 25 countries and regions. In 2012 ibis Styles was established with the re-branding of the former All Seasons properties.

ibis (*red logo*) represents Accor's largest portfolio of hotels and resorts with 1,047 hotels in 61 countries and regions. From 1997, ibis was the first economy hotel brand to be quality certified ISO 9001, an international standard outlining its commitment to service quality. 85% of the network is ISO 9001 certified. Ibis is a standard brand equivalent to two to three-star hotels.

Midscale brands

Mercure (美居) is the largest of Accor's midscale brands found internationally with 732 hotels and resorts in 55 countries and regions.

Novotel (诺富特) has 414 full-service hotels and resorts in 61 countries. **Suite Novotel** has 31 all-suite hotels in 10 countries and regions.

Adagio offers 96 "ready-to-live" apartment-style accommodations in 11 countries and regions suitable for medium and long-stay business guests. The Adagio aparthotel (apartment hotel) brand is divided into two segments with upscale called Adagio city apartments and midscale called Adagio Access city apartments. Adagio is a joint partnership between Accor hotels and Pierre & Vacances tourism.

Upscale brands

Grand Mercure (美爵) is a full-service hotel and resort brand representing 15 hotels and apartment hotels in 8 countries.

Grand Mercure Apartments cater to long-stay travellers with rates that depend on length of stay. The apartments have kitchen and laundrette facilities. There are 15 apartments in 4 countries.

Mei Jue is a Chinese adaptation of the Grand Mercure brand. It is designed for travellers in China who want an upscale hotel brand. There are 14 hotels and more than 65 new developments scheduled for 2015.

Maha Cipta is the Indonesian adaptation of Grand Mercure. It has two hotels in Indonesia.

The Sebel is a brand of premium apartments. There are 21 properties in Australia and New Zealand.

Appendix 1
Hotel Groups 酒店集团

Mama Shelter is a design-oriented lifestyle chain of boutique hotels. (The chief designer of Mama Shelter hotels is world-renowned Philippe Starck). Accor acquired a 35% stake in Mama Shelter in October 2014. In April 2015, Mama Shelter had six hotels in Bordeaux, Istanbul, Los Angeles, Lyon, Marseille and Paris. The chain's five-year pipeline includes properties in Amsterdam, Barcelona, Lille (France), London, Mexico City, New York City, Seoul and a second Parisian hotel.

Pullman (铂尔曼) has 99 upscale hotels and resorts in 28 countries.

MGallery is a collection of 77 high-end boutique hotels in 23 countries and regions. The brand's official Ambassador is actress Kristin Scott Thomas.

Swissotel Hotels are soon to be part of Accor's upscale brand due to AccorHotels & FRHI merger. Until merger transaction finalized in 2016, FRHI and AccorHotels will continue to operate its brands as separate companies and manage their business affairs as usual.

Luxury brands

Sofitel (索菲特) is Accor's luxury hotel and resort brand with 121 hotels in 41 countries and regions.

SO Sofitel are designer hotels in Bangkok, Thailand, Bel Ombre, Mauritius and Singapore. Each SO is designed by a famous fashion designer: Kenzo Takada designed the SO Sofitel Mauritius, Christian Lacroix designed the SO Sofitel Bangkok and Isabelle Miaja designed the SO Sofitel Singapore.

Sofitel Legend is a chain of hotels in five countries. The hotels are usually listed as historic monuments. These include Sofitel Legend Metropole in Hanoi (Vietnam), Sofitel Legend, the Grand Amsterdam (Netherlands), Sofitel Old Cataract in Aswan (Egypt), Sofitel Cartagena Santa Clara (Colombia) and Sofitel People's Grand Hotel of Xi'an (China).

Raffles Hotels and Fairmont Hotels are soon to be part of Accor's ultra-luxury brand due to AccorHotels & FRHI merger. Until merger transaction finalized in 2016, FRHI and AccorHotels will continue to operate its brands as separate companies and manage their business affairs.

Advertisemment

We built smile! 我们创造微笑！（ACCOR）

Suite hotel. A new way of hotel living. 雅高套房饭店。一种新的酒店生活。(Suite hotel)

NOVOTEL. Contemporary hotel concept convenient for business and leisure. 诺富特酒店，方便、休闲的现代商务酒店。(Novotel)

American chain of economy motels. 美国连锁的经济型汽车旅馆。(Red Roof)

Budget hotels offering simple and functional comfort. 经济型酒店提供简单实用的舒适体验。(F1)

Round-the-clock service and budget prices. 我们有24小时的服务和低价收费。(Ibis)

Mercure. For the best of the region. 美居酒店，做本地最好的。(Mercure)

7. Choice Hotels International, Inc（美国精品国际酒店集团）

Choice Hotels International, Inc. is an American hospitality holding corporation based in Rockville, Maryland, in the United States. The company owns the hotel and motel brands Comfort Inn, Comfort Suites, Quality Inn, Sleep Inn, Clarion, Cambria Hotel & Suites, Mainstay Suites, Suburban Extended Stay, Econo Lodge, Rodeway Inn and Ascend Hotel Collection. The company manages 6,379 properties worldwide. There are 505,278 rooms, with approximately $45.80 in revenue per room, totaling $758 million in revenue as of April, 2016.

Headquarters relocation

In October 2010, officials in Maryland and Montgomery County announced that Choice Hotels International would move its headquarters from suburban Silver Spring to Rockville, about 20 minutes northwest of its current location in 2013. Choice Hotels' new headquarters is now located in Rockville Town Center.

In August 2011, Choice Hotels broke ground on its 197,866 square feet (18,382.4 m^2) corporate headquarters in Rockville.

Brands

Choice Hotels includes the brands: Ascend Hotel Collection, Cambria Hotels & Suites, Clarion Hotels, Clarion Suites, Comfort Inn/Comfort Inn & Suites, Comfort Suites, Econo Lodge, Mainstay Suites, Quality Inn/Hotel/Quality Inn & Suites, Rodeway Inn, Sleep Inn/Sleep Inn & Suites, Suburban Extended Stay Hotel.

8. Best Western International, Inc.（最佳西方国际集团）

Best Western International, Inc., operator of the Best Western Hotels & Resorts brand, operates about 4,100 hotels and motels. The chain, with its corporate headquarters in Phoenix, Arizona, operates 2,163 hotels in North America. The brand was founded by M.K. Geurtin in 1946. David Kong is the president and CEO of Best Western, and Dorothy Dowling is the chief marketing officer.

In 1964, Best Western took the first step towards global expansion when Canadian hotel owners joined the system. Best Western then expanded to Mexico, Australia and New Zealand in 1976.

In 2002, Best Western International launched Best Western Premier in Europe and Asia. (The other hotels in the chain were known as Best Western.) In 2011, the chain's branding system-wide changed to a three-tiered system: Best Western, Best Western Plus and Best Western Premier. Since it no longer operates under a single brand, Best Western concurrently modified its slogan in 2011 from "the world's largest hotel chain" to "the world's largest hotel family".

Business model

Best Western charges its franchisees a rate that is based on an initial cost plus a fee for each additional room. Best Western also publishes a list of standards that each hotel needs to maintain.

The hotels are allowed to keep their independent identity. Though they must use Best Western signage and identify themselves as a Best Western hotel, the hotels are allowed the option of using their own independent name as part of their identity (for example *Best Western Adobe Inn*, in Santa Rosa, New Mexico or the *Best Western Berkshire Inn*, in Bethel, Connecticut).

In the US, the properties can either be traditional roadside motels, motor inns or full-service hotels. There are also many smaller "mini-chains" that are owned by the same management within Best Western; for example at one time the Best Western Midway Hotels found in the Midwestern United States. Outside the United States, the properties are mainly hotels. More than 90 percent of Best Western hotels in Europe have three or four-star ratings.

Best Western provides reservation and brand identity services for all of its worldwide hotels. It has multilingual reservation centers in Phoenix and Milan, Italy.

In the United Kingdom, an additional service fee is imposed on telephone bookings through the use of a premium rate telephone number.

Differentiation

In 2011, Best Western changed its branding chain-wide (after starting a similar idea in 2002 in some areas of Europe and Asia) with three levels of progressively more amenities and features: *Best Western*, *Best Western Plus* and *Best Western Premier*. A Best Western can have the basics, e.g. an in-room coffeemaker, free local calls, available breakfast, cable television and free WiFi, etc. A Best Western Plus would have those amenities of a Best Western plus a fitness room, swimming pool, business room and onsite laundry room. A Best Western Premier would have all those amenities plus onsite dining, high-quality furnishings, premium towels and bath products, an onsite shop for snacks or essentials, meeting rooms and an LCD television with HD channels.

9. Huazhu Hotels Group Ltd.（华住酒店集团）

Huazhu Hotels Group Ltd. is a hotel management company in China. It was previously known in English as China Lodging Group Limited (NasdaQ：HTHT). The company head office is in Changning District, Shanghai.

The China Lodging/Hanting Inns business was established in 2005. The original company,

Powerhill, was established in 2005, and the current Huazhu company was established in 2007. Ji Qi (季琦), the founder, stated that he got the idea to start the chain by reading a book discussing Accor Hotels. As of 2012 the company had four brands and about 1,000 properties in China.

In May 2015 the company announced that former President Jenny Zhang was to be appointed Chief Executive Officer.

Operations

The company brands include **Hanting Inns and Hotels** (汉庭连锁酒店) including **Hanting Express** (汉庭快捷), **Hi Inn** (海友酒店), **JI Hotel** (全季酒店), **Starway Hotel** (星程酒店), **Joya Hotel** (禧玥), and **Manxin Hotels and Resorts** (漫心度假酒店). The company classifies Joya and Manxin as upscale brands, JI and Starway as midscale, and Hanting and Hi Inn as economy brands. Previously the sub-brands of Hanting Inns and Hotels were **Hanting Seasons Hotel**, **Hanting Express Hotel and Hanting Hi Inn**.

Jiazhen Huo and Zhisheng Hong, authors of *Service Science in China*, wrote that the Hanting brand is promoted to be "similar to youth' hostels so as to meet the customer demands lower than its former market positioning".

10. Hyatt Hotels Corporation（凯悦酒店集团）

Hyatt Hotels Corporation is an American multinational owner, operator, franchiser of hotels, resorts and vacation properties. The Hyatt Corporation came into being upon purchase of the Hyatt House, at Los Angeles International Airport, on September 27, 1957. In 2016, *Fortune* magazine listed Hyatt as the 47th-best U.S. company to work for.

Full-service lodging

- **Park Hyatt** (柏悦) are residential luxury Hyatt hotels, mid-sized hotels in cities considered premier destinations.
- **Andaz** (安达仕) hotels are upscale lifestyle boutique-style hotels.
- **Grand Hyatt** (君悦) hotels are large luxury hotels in major cities and holiday destinations.
- **Hyatt Regency** (凯悦) is Hyatt's flagship hotel brand that are mid to large scaled premium hotels intended for both leisure and business travelers, including those attending conventions, located in urban, suburban, airport, convention and resort destinations around the world.
- **Hyatt** hotels are smaller full-service hotels with 150 to 350 rooms located close to major business centers.
- **Hyatt Centric** is a new, full service lifestyle brand designed for business and leisure travelers.

Select-service lodging
- **Hyatt Place** (凯悦嘉轩) hotels are mid-sized hotels catering for family.

Extended-stay lodging
- **Hyatt House** (凯悦嘉寓) (formerly known as Hyatt Summerfield Suites or Summerfield Suites by Wyndham and Hotel Sierra) properties are extended-stay residential hotels and smaller-to-mid-sized modern hotels in urban and suburban locations in the United States.

All-inclusive resorts
- **Hyatt Zilara** and **Hyatt Ziva** hotels are all-inclusive resorts. Zilara does not accommodate children.

Timeshares
- **Hyatt Residence Club** are timeshare properties with the same service as the Hyatt brand.

11. Kempinski Hotels S.A. (凯宾斯基酒店集团)

Kempinski Hotels S.A. is an international hotel chain founded as the Hotelbetriebs-Aktiengesellschaft in Berlin, Germany, in 1897. The Corporate Office is located in Geneva, Switzerland. Thailand's Crown Property Bureau (CPB Equity Co. Ltd) has the majority holding in the group.

Corporate ownership

The parallel history of the present-day hotel company began in 1897 with the foundation of the *Hotelbetriebs-Aktiengesellschaft* in Berlin by the banker Leopold Koppel. In 1926, the company was taken over by *Aschinger*, who also ran the *Hotel Kaiserhof* and the *Hotel Baltic*.

When in 1953 Friedrich Unger sold his shares and the name Kempinski to the *Hotelbetriebs-Aktiengesellschaft*, the name Bristol was adopted. In subsequent years, the "Hotelbetriebs-Aktiengesellschaft" took over the management of several hotels. In 1957, it acquired the *Hotel Atlantic* in Hamburg. This elegant hotel, known as *Weisses Schloss* ("White Castle"), was opened in 1909 and was a recognized Hamburg institution even then.

In 1970, the General Assembly of the *Hotelbetriebs-Aktiengesellschaft* voted to change its name to *Kempinski Hotelbetriebs- Aktiengesellschaft*. In the same year, a long-lasting partnership was established with Lufthansa in the form of a 50-percent participation in the *Hotel Vier*

Jahreszeiten in Munich, in which Lufthansa already had a holding. In 1977, the hotel company received its present name as *Kempinski Aktiengesellschaft (AG)*. At the same time, the *Kempinski Hotel Gravenbruch* in Frankfurt was added to the group's portfolio as its fourth German hotel.

In 1985, Lufthansa acquired shares in *Kempinski AG* and thereby enabled the hotel company to operate Kempinski hotels abroad too. A year later, *Kempinski AG*, Lufthansa and the finance company *Rolaco S.A.* founded *Kempinski Hotels S.A.*, with its head office in Geneva. In 1993 *Kempinski AG* acquired all the shares in *Kempinski S.A.*

The Dusit Sindhorn Company Ltd. took over Kempinski in November 1994, when it acquired a 52% stake. The 50:50 joint venture between Dusit Thani Group and the Siam Commercial Bank eventually accumulated a 83% stake in the group, and Dusit Thani exited from the joint venture in 1998, when it sold out to its partner.

Advertisememnt

The access to success. 生意成功的方向。(Kempinski, Beijing)

12. Four Seasons Hotels and Resorts（四季酒店管理集团）

Four Seasons Hotels Ltd., trading as Four Seasons Hotels and Resorts, is a Canadian international luxury, five-star hospitality company. *Travel+Leisure* magazine and Zagat Survey rank the hotel chain's 98 properties among the top luxury hotels worldwide. Readers of *Conde Nast Traveler* magazine have voted Four Seasons Tented Camp Golden Triangle in Chiang Rai, Thailand as among the top ten hotels in the world for three consecutive years. The company has been named one of the "100 Best Companies to Work For" by *Fortune* every year since the survey's inception in 1998, ranking No. 47 in 2015, and is lauded for having one of the lowest employee turnover rates in the hospitality industry.

Business model

Four Seasons does not own most of its properties; it operates them on behalf of real estate owners and developers. The contracts between Four Seasons and property owners typically permit the company to participate in the design of the property and run it with nearly total control over every aspect of the operation.

Four Seasons generally earns 3 percent of the gross income and approximately 5 percent of profits from the properties it operates, and the property owners are required to additionally contribute money for chain-wide sales, marketing and reservations systems. Four Seasons hotels have larger staffs than competing chains, therefore they create separate reserve accounts to cover upkeep costs. While profit margins are relatively low, the reputation of the brand and the value of the hotel for sale as well as loan collateral generates developer interest. Four Seasons also produces a complimentary magazine for guests that is supported by advertising revenue. Four Seasons has a fractional ownership division, Four Seasons Residence Clubs.

Residential Rentals

Four Seasons Hotels and Resorts expanded their business into vacation rentals, titled Residential Rentals, in June 2014. These rentals are available in:

- North America (Costa Rica, Houston, Jackson Hole, Nevis, Punta Mita, San Diego, Whistler, Vail)
- Africa (Marrakech, Mauritius, Seychelles, Sharm El Sheikh)
- Europe (Cap-Ferrat)
- Asia (Jimbaran Bay, Chiang Mai, Koh Samui)

The model of Residential Rentals is based on providing the same services as Four Seasons Hotels and Resorts in a residential setting. They were created as a way to target multi-generational and small group travel according to Jose Sorian, the VP of Worldwide Residential Operations for Four Seasons Hotels and Resorts.

13. Mandarin Oriental Hotel Group（文华东方酒店集团）

Mandarin Oriental Hotel Group, a member of the Jardine Matheson Group, is an international hotel investment and management group with luxury hotels, resorts and residences in Asia, Europe and the Americas.

History

Although 1876 was the "official" opening year of the Oriental Hotel, the origin of the "Oriental" side of the Mandarin Oriental can be traced back as early as 1863, when two Americans, Captain Atkins Dyer and William West, opened the Oriental Hotel in Bangkok, Siam (now Thailand): however, the original building burnt down only two years later, on 11 June 1865.

However, the history of the "Mandarin" side of the group is comparatively recent: the Mandarin hotel only opened in 1963, in the Central District of Hong Kong Island. In 1973, the Excelsior Hotel, which continues to use a separate brand today, opened in Causeway Bay.

In 1974, Mandarin International Hotels Limited was formed as a hotel management company, with the intention was to expand into Asia. That year, the company acquired a 49% interest in the Oriental Hotel, resulting in two "flagship" hotels for the company.

In 1985, the Company combined the two hotels under a common name, Mandarin Oriental Hotel Group. In 1987, Mandarin Oriental Hotel Group was floated on the Stock Exchange of Hong Kong under the name of "Mandarin Oriental International Limited". Mandarin Oriental International Limited, is incorporated in Bermuda, and listed in London, Singapore and Bermuda. Mandarin Oriental Hotel Group Limited, which operates from Hong Kong, manages the activities of the Group's hotels.

Mandarin Oriental Hotel Group operates, or has under development, 41 hotels representing over 10,000 rooms in 27 countries and regions, with 18 hotels in Asia, 12 in the Americas and 12 in Europe and North Africa. In addition, the Group operates, or has under development, 13 Residences at Mandarin Oriental, connected to the Group's properties.

14. Shangri-La Hotels and Resorts（香格里拉酒店集团）

Shangri-La Hotels and Resorts is a Hong Kong-based multinational hospitality company. Founded by Robert Kuok in 1971, the company has 111 hotels and resorts with over 38,000 rooms in Asia, Europe, Middle East, North America and Australia.

Shangri-La has 5 brands across different market segments including Shangri-La Hotels, Shangri-La Resorts, Traders Hotels, Kerry Hotels and Hotel Jen. The five-star luxury lodgings of the chain can be found across Asia, the Middle East, Canada, Oceania and Europe.

The first hotel of the luxury Shangri-La group was the Shangri-La Hotel Singapore, opened in 1971. The name refers to the fictional place Shangri-La, described in the 1933 novel *Lost Horizon* by British author James Hilton.

15. Langham Hotels International（朗廷酒店集团）

Langham Hospitality Group is a luxury hotels operator dating back to 1865, when The Langham, London originally opened as Europe's first "Grand Hotel".

Today, the group covers four continents, with projects located in cities and resorts around the world, including Auckland, Bahamas, Bangkok, Beijing, Boston, Guangzhou, Hong Kong, London, Los Angeles, Melbourne, Phuket, Pune, Samui and Shanghai. The group's rapid expansion continues with its two brands, the Langham and Langham Place, as well as its affiliate brand Eaton.

Langham Hotels International is wholly owned by the Great Eagle Group, one of Hong Kong's leading property companies, which was founded in 1963 and is now listed on the Hong Kong Stock Exchange.

Company

Langham Hotels International is a wholly owned subsidiary of the Great Eagle Hospitality Group. It not only oversees the operations and performance of its own hotels, but also provides professional management services to its developer-or owner-partners.

The Great Eagle Hospitality Group is the hospitality arm of Great Eagle Holdings Limited. One of Hong Kong's leading property and hotel companies, Great Eagle Holdings invests in, develops and manages office, retail, residential and hotel properties in Asia, North America and Europe. The organisation is also active in property management and maintenance services as well as building materials trading.

Great Eagle Holdings was founded in 1963 with the incorporation of the Great Eagle Company Limited, which was listed on the Hong Kong Stock Exchange in 1972. In 1990, following a reorganisation, Great Eagle Holdings Limited, incorporated in Bermuda, became the listed holding company of Great Eagle in place of the Great Eagle Company Limited.

The Great Eagle Hospitality Group has an extensive hotel portfolio with over 5,000 rooms, virtually all of them managed by Langham Hotels International.

The group's collection of hotels currently in operations consists of nine luxury properties across four continents: including Auckland, Boston, Hong Kong, London, Melbourne, Los Angeles, Shanghai and Thailand.

Eaton Hotels represents the third and more accessible brand under Great Eagle Hospitality. The Group additionally owns the 1,590-room Chelsea Hotel in Toronto.

Brands

- The Langham Hotels and Resorts
- Langham Place Hotels and Resorts
- Eaton Hotels (affiliate brand)
- Eaton House
- Chuan Spa

Appendix 2　Skills and Abilities for Hotel 酒店业技能与能力

1. Skills

Skills are very important to work in the hotel. Skills mean an ability that has been acquired by training. We could basically master our skills by more training or practice. A skill also means the ability to apply knowledge and use them in order to perform better to complete tasks and solve problems. Skills are described as "Cognitive" (involving the use of logical, creative thinking) or "Practical" (involving manual dexterity and the use of methods, materials, tools and instruments).

Here are some lists of skills which are essential for hospitality industry.

(1) Speaking: This skill means talking to others to convey information effectively. It is very important in the hotel to convey correct information in understandable tone, polite and efficient way every time. Speaking is very important not only to convey message to guests but also to perform well in other aspects and share and convey inter-departmental messages. To have effective team and to show team spirit and great result, speaking or communication is very important. Speaking in the hotel must be common and understandable to every staff. Everyone must use one language to convey or share their thoughts or ideas.

(2) Active listening: We must at all time listen to others carefully to know what they want and what their demands or requests are. Active listening is another most important skill in the hotel. It means to give full attention to what other people are saying. While you are listening you must take time to understand the points being made. If necessary, ask questions as appropriate to make sure that you understand completely. While asking questions you must not interrupt at inappropriate times. You have to be focused at all times and make sure that nothing is missed out in conversation.

(3) Service orientation: Service is very important in hotel. At all times we must be active and enthusiastic about helping others or thinking about how to make others satisfy—service orientation doesn't necessarily mean to serve the customer and make them satisfy; it's the whole working process around you. No matter they are customers, colleagues, or staff from other departments, we always need to be active and look for ways to help others. This will definitely make work place harmonious and work environment better. When we have better environment we can perform better and achieve goals easily.

(4) Social perceptiveness: In our daily work in hotel we encounter many situations and different people from around the world. We everyday see so many actions, signs and different ways of performing the same thing. In this situation we must be aware of others' reactions and understand why they react as they do. We must be able to understand things easily and quickly on others' performance. We must understand others' cultures and ways of doing things and never

make fun of or laugh at their ways. As to have a great team we must understand each other and create a better working place to provide better service.

(5) Coordination: It's hard for a single person to achieve or fulfill everything that the guests request at one time. It's even harder for a single person to do each and every thing without making a plan. While working we must skillfully organize the people or things in order to make them work together effectively. We must adjust our actions in relation to others' actions. We must prioritize our work and deal with them one after another to complete the whole task.

(6) Interpersonal skills: The ability to create good relationships between yourself and other people is called interpersonal skills. If you don't have good relationship with others, you won't be able to work well and provide excellent service to your customers. Being kind to others, talking politely, always having smile on face, keeping an eye contact at all times are some important ones.

(7) Emotional intelligence: The ability to recognize and control your emotions to maintain a high level of professionalism with internal staff and external customers is very important. At all times we have to provide excellent service with commitment without being disturbed by our own problems or emotions.

(8) Instructing: In our daily life we have to do a lot of things to fulfill our duty. As saying goes, "nobody is perfect", we must learn from others. This skill teaches others how to do things and be better. We must practice every day and learn to share with others. While instructing others we must follow the standards and procedures provided by the hotel at all times.

(9) Active learning: Learning is a life-long process. Every day while we work we need to understand and learn many things. We must try to understand the implications of new information for both current and future problem-solving and decision-making. We must at all time use logic and reasons to identify the strengths and weaknesses of alternative solutions, for which we must always try to find new solutions, materials or ideas. That's how we can create smooth work environment.

(10) Problem solving: We face lots of problems in our daily work. When we face those problems we must handle them with care and solve them as soon as possible. While solving problems we must think of alternatives and its consequences. Understanding communication, knowledge of products, innovativeness, and creativeness are very important while solving problem.

(11) Decision making: Making decision is another important skill in the hotel. While making decision we must consider the best way to transmit our decision. We must have a good communication channel while letting others know. We must also consider who will be affected by the decision and what likely effect will be on them. We must also anticipate obstacles and objections while making decision. Critical thinking is very important before making decision. We also need to have alternative plans or plan B. If something goes wrong or doesn't work out we should be prepared to formulate or change the decision.

(12) Job task planning and organizing: Each and every member of the hotel staff has their

responsibilities. The entire task must be organized and planned better beforehand. We must follow the standard all the time and complete entire task. We should have knowledge to utilize methods and organization techniques to ensure efficiency and respect others.

(13) Finding information: We do encounter lots of problems and need to find solutions every day. When we don't get help around we must know how to find the information ourselves. Being curious and trying to come up with new and better idea in workplace is very important. If we were more enthusiastic and innovative about our work, we could handle situation better and faster. It is so essential to find relevant information to clarify and provide better answer or information to customers or colleagues.

2. Abilities

Abilities are often thought of as innate. Everyone has different abilities and we should find out about them and know how to take advantage of them.

(1) Ability to work under pressure: We must know how to deal with pressure while working. We must develop a working habit where we can deal with it in efficient ways. Especially at peak hour when a lot of activities happening around you, you must know how to manage and work in order.

(2) Ability to learn: No one expects you to know it all in the beginning, but we must listen and learn all times. If you don't know, ask questions until you are clear about it. We all learn from mistakes but try to avoid making same mistakes again and again. Always show your concern and try to improve yourself with more knowledge, procedures and rules.

(3) Oral expression and speech clarity: We must talk to people every day to convey our messages or listen to theirs. Oral expression is the ability to communicate information and ideas in speaking so that others will understand. We must express ourselves clearly in understandable language. We must speak slowly, politely and in normal pace so others can understand us. We should always sound natural.

(4) Speech recognition: When we talk to other people we must have an ability to identify and understand the speech of another person at all time. We must know how to appreciate others and express gratitude for the suggestions, ideas or thoughts. We should always respect others' opinion and show our acknowledgment to them.

(5) Information ordering: We all have our own way of working or dealing with things. Some people are better at this while others need to pay extra attention to this. The ability to arrange things or actions in certain order or pattern according to specific rule or standard of the hotel is very important to work efficiently and quickly.

(6) Problem sensitivity: While we work we must keep our eye open and pay attention to each and every little things. We must have the ability to tell when something is wrong or is likely to go wrong. If we could have this sense we could avoid lots of trouble in work.

(7) Arm-Hand steadiness and trunk strength: Health is very important to everyone. We must

at all time take care of our health and eat healthy. Working in the hotel you must have a good health condition especially trunk strength and arm steadiness. Some people naturally have strong heath condition while others not. We must eat healthy food and do regular exercise at all times.

3. Work Styles

There are many styles of work that we carry in hotel. While at work we must understand and respect the aspects of work and follow the standard and complete the task. This doesn't mean how to work in the hotel but it means while we are at work what the things that we should keep in mind are. If we follow this at all time, this will make our work easier. This will teach you how to perform better.

(1) Self-control: When we work in the hotel we must maintain our composure. We must at all time keep our emotions and anger in control. At all times we have to avoid aggressive behavior. We must and should control ourselves at all times.

(2) Cooperation: While working we must be pleasant to others and must display cooperative attitude. We must help each other and should know how to take advantage of the situation for shared common goals. We must keep our differences aside for the company's standard procedure and customer's satisfaction.

(3) Social orientation: We can't complete all tasks by working alone. We must prefer to work with others rather than alone. Team work should be given the first priority for everyone. At work we must personally connect with others to create good work environment. We should put our personal ego aside and work for the best outcome.

(4) Integrity: While we work we must be trustworthy and should always act with integrity. We always must be honest and admit our mistakes and avoid telling lies. At all times we must give straight answers to all questions.

(5) Adaptability/Flexibility: We must adapt to the change whether they are positive or negative. We must be flexible at all times. Every customer and every day is different. We must be open to change. We must consider variety in the workplace and deal with them calmly.

(6) Attention to detail: No matter where you work, which department you work in, back of the house or front of the house, you must be careful about every detail and through in completing the task that is yours. Every small things matter. Every job is important, hence every job must be completely done.

(7) Stress tolerance: While we work we get lots of criticism and suggestions, at those moments we must accept them and deal with them calmly and effectively. We should always be patient and positive for every situation.

4. Personal Attributes and Skills

(1) Reliability: People can rely on you. You should respect the time and be punctual.

(2) Commonsense: At all time take logic approach to tasks. Always think before you act and don't be impulsive.

(3) Initiative: Take interest in each and every task. Ask questions if you get stuck. Show your enthusiasm to each task.

(4) Organization and time management: You must be able to plan, prioritize and manage your time.

(5) Honesty: Always be trustworthy and act with integrity. Always answer straight, admit your mistakes and show your willingness to learn from them. Be true to yourself.

(6) Enthusiasm: Always show positive attitude and motivation towards work. Act like you are enjoying yourself.

(7) Commitment: Always take the responsibility of work seriously and focus on your work rather than other stuffs which are bothering you. Show your interest in task you do daily.

(8) Well-groomed appearance: Always present yourself in neat and clean dressup. Ensure that your hair, nails and shoes are clean. Always practice good hygiene.

(9) Positive self-esteem: Always hold yourself confident and have a belief in your worth.

(10) Problem solving: Solve problem swiftly to satisfy your customer and employer. Be cautious while solving and make sure it doesn't happen again.

(11) Communication skills: Communicate clearly with customers, colleagues and employers. Understand others' needs and wants and present yourself in understandable way.

(12) Sense of humor: Don't be serious and take things seriously. See the light side of things but don't act like the clown. Always enjoy the task and present yourself with smile.

(13) Adaptability: Be flexible and open to change.

(14) Loyalty: Respect your employer and colleagues at all times. Do not bad mouth anyone and respect confidential things. Do not share confidential things with others.

(15) Ability to work under pressure: Cope with pressure with positive attitude and always be calm and have fun with it.

(16) Customer service: Always attend to the needs and wants of the customers. Always focus on how to exceed their expectations.

(17) Teamwork: Work with the team or lead the team at all times. Work for common goal rather than personal means.

(18) Ability to learn: Listen and learn, ask questions if you have doubts. Learn from your mistakes and try not to repeat them.

(19) Computer skills: Technology plays a bigger role in hospitality. You must have basic computer knowledge and know how to use them for you own benefits.

Appendix 3 Duties of Different Positions in the Hotel
酒店的工作岗位及其职责

1. Receptionist

A Hotel Receptionist job involves dealing with guests on a daily basis. As you work on this field you will check in and check out guests. Take reservations as part of administration work and offering valuable information regarding accommodation and services. Some of their responsibilities are as follows in most of the international chain hotel brands but are not limited.

(1) Prepare useful papers, equipment and forms for daily necessary work.

(2) Maintain reception area and back area.

(3) Meet hotel attendance and grooming standards.

(4) Maintain current hotel information to be able to provide information to guests.

(5) Receiving and registering guests as they arrive.

(6) Greet the customer and identify his specific reservation.

(7) Register the guest, ensuring that the necessary details are obtained, i.e. name in full, address, whether company or private booking, special rate, VIP, charge details, nationality, passport number, etc.

(8) Allocate room according to reservations list, ensuring that this is what the guest has booked, both in terms of the room itself and the rate to be paid.

(9) Issue the key card.

(10) Fill out necessary form and file it for future references.

(11) Create guest history report as per hotel requirement.

(12) Receive the payment for accommodation.

(13) Liaise or alert concierge so that the guest's luggage is taken to his room.

(14) Keep records in designated place.

(15) Update occupancy list, arrival guest list, in-house guest list.

(16) Be on hand to book and make the call the appropriate time if the client requires to book a wake-up call.

(17) Take care and maintain of all the equipment and asserts.

(18) Maintain knowledge of special programs and events in the hotel in order to recognize and respond to guests needs.

(19) Maintain a high level of product and service knowledge in order to explain and sell services and facilities to guests.

(20) Ensure that all departments, particularly restaurants are notified of the tariff entitlements.

(21) Receive mails and direct them to the guests in the hotel.

(22) Complete office bulletin book.

(23) Communicate well to ensure effective shift hand-over.

(24) Handle guest requests.

(25) Safe keeping of client valuables. Keep client valuables safe.

(26) Keep area clean and tidy.

(27) Maintain confidentiality.

(28) Implements department procedures and policies as needed.

(29) Attend to all briefings.

(30) Participate in training.

(31) Demonstrate awareness of hotel policies and procedures and ensure all procedures are conducted safely and within the guidelines.

(32) Be aware of duty of care and adhere to occupational, health and safety legislation, policies and procedures.

(33) Be familiar with property safety, first aid and fire and emergency procedures and operate equipment safely and sensibly.

(34) Initiate action to correct a hazardous situation and notify supervisors of potential dangers.

(35) Strive for constant improvement and take responsibility for your own performance.

(36) Adhere to Hotel Handbook and general policies and procedures.

(37) Provide information when requested and promotes hotel's services, facilities and special events.

(38) Build and maintain positive relationships with all internal customers and guests in order to anticipate their needs.

(39) Anticipate guest needs, handle guest enquires, and solve problems.

(40) Create a positive hotel image in every interaction with internal and external customers.

(41) Adhere to hotel brand standards.

(42) Demonstrate co-operation and trust with colleagues, supervisors, teams and across departments.

(43) Actively participate in organized meetings.

(44) Interact with department and hotel staff in a professional and positive manner to foster good rapport, promote team spirit and ensure two way communication effective.

(45) Be open to new ideas and make changes in the job and routine as required.

(46) Work in line with business requirements.

(47) Develop/update skills and knowledge (internally or externally) to reflect changed technology or changed work requirements.

(48) Seek feedback on areas of shortfall.

(49) Maximize opportunities for self-development.

Appendix 3

Duties of Different Positions in the Hotel 酒店的工作岗位及其职责

(50) Ensure that your work quality meets the standards required and complete tasks in a timely and thorough manner with minimum supervision.

(51) Follow standards, policies and procedures.

2. Bell Boy

A bell boy is someone employed in a hotel for the purpose of carrying luggage for the guests as they come or leave the hotel. He should as he welcomes them, go on to show them and escort them to their respective rooms. He may also run errands that may arise in the hotel, during his shift. Their responsibilities will include, but not limited to the following.

(1) Make sure that working area is clean and tidy.

(2) Open the front door for guests (in some hotels).

(3) Meet/greet guests with hotel standards.

(4) Load and unload luggage from the vehicles that the clients either come in with or are leaving in.

(5) Transport baggage to guest room.

(6) Provide valet service on request (in some hotel valet service is an individual department but in some hotel it is provided by the bell boy).

(7) Control standards of service procedures.

(8) Maintain baggage tags.

(9) Delivery newspaper to every room in the morning.

(10) Store bags.

(11) Open room doors.

(12) Give directions on request.

(13) Call taxis if requested.

(14) Assist guests and escort them to locations within the hotel at their request.

(15) Make sure that trollies are always on good condition and available.

(16) Maintain the caddy and its conditions (if required).

(17) Arrange transport to airport or airport pick up.

(18) Report any maintenance job.

(19) To book a wake-up call, the bell boy needs to be on hand to book and make the call at the appropriate time (in some hotel wake-up call is organized by the reception desk or receptionist).

(20) Maintain knowledge of special programs and events in the hotel in order to recognize and respond to guests needs.

(21) Anticipate guest needs, handle guest enquires, and solve problems.

(22) Follow standards, policies and procedures.

(23) Demonstrate awareness of hotel policies and procedures and ensure all procedures are conducted safely and within the guidelines.

(24) Be aware of duty of care and adhere to occupational, health and safety legislation, policies and procedures.

(25) Be familiar with property safety, first aid, fire and emergency procedures and operate equipment safely and sensibly.

(26) Initiate actions to correct a hazardous situation and notify supervisors of potential dangers.

(27) Strive for constant improvement and take responsibility for your own performance.

(28) Adhere to Hotel Handbook and general policies and procedures.

(29) Provide information when requested and promote hotel's services, facilities and special events.

(30) Build and maintain positive relationships with all internal customers and guests in order to anticipate their needs.

(31) Create a positive hotel image in every interaction with internal and external customers.

(32) Adhere to hotel brand standards.

(33) Assist guests and escort them to locations within the hotel at their request.

(34) Demonstrate co-operation and trust with colleagues, supervisors, teams and across departments.

(35) Actively participate in organized meetings.

(36) Interact with department and hotel staff in a professional and positive manner to foster good rapport, promote team spirit and ensure two way communication effective.

(37) Be open to new ideas and make changes in the job and routine as required.

(38) Work in line with business requirements.

(39) Develop/update skills and knowledge (internally or externally) to reflect changed technology or changed work requirements.

(40) Seek feedback on areas of shortfall.

(41) Maximize opportunities for self-development.

(42) Ensure that your work quality meets the standards required and complete tasks in a timely and thorough manner with minimum supervision.

(43) Follow standards, policies and procedures.

(44) Work effectively with customers and colleagues from different viewpoints and cultures.

3. Waiter and Waitress

Food-service workers perform an important job that is always in demand. Waiters at restaurants have a responsibility to serve the customers' needs during the time they are in the restaurant. Their duties and responsibilities will include, but not limited to the following.

(1) Clean agreed designated areas, in accordance with the hotel procedures, morning/evening routines and hygiene requirements.

Appendix 3

Duties of Different Positions in the Hotel 酒店的工作岗位及其职责

(2) Change table linen as required and ensure dirty or damaged linen is counted and exchanged for clean, usable items.

(3) Clean and refill cruet and condiment sets.

(4) Ensure that flowers and table decorations are flesh and comply with agreed standards.

(5) Set tables according to the standard, ensuring that all items used are clean, undamaged and in a good state of repair.

(6) Ensure sideboards on stations are adequately stocked with replacement cutlery, linen or other necessary items for service period.

(7) Prepare salads, sandwiches, cheese boards and coffee according to the standards, when this is an agreed duty of the establishment (But in some hotel waiters don't have to prepare anything).

(8) Take orders from customers and ensure these are given to the appropriate person (in some hotel waiters don't have to take orders).

(9) Inform customers of daily specials, chef specials or any other promotional items.

(10) Anticipate guest needs, handle guest enquires, and solve problem.

(11) Upsell food and beverage products in the department at all times.

(12) Provide information when requested and promote hotel's service, facilities and special events.

(13) Be totally familiar with the composition of all menu items including wines, foods and beverages.

(14) Serve food and beverage in accordance with the hotel standard, but above all in a professional, and courteous manner.

(15) Clean tables and ensure they are cleaned as soon as it is apparent that customers have finished their food or drink with an acceptable balance between speed, yet allowing customers to finish their meal without feeling rushed.

(16) Ensure that customers are correctly charged, present the bill and take payment from the customer, in accordance with the procedures of the establishment.

(17) At all times be aware of and practice good customer relations, assisting the guest in any way which does not adversely affect other customers.

(18) Attend to customer complaints satisfactorily.

(19) Carry out on-the-job training to ensure subordinate staff can carry out their duties effectively.

(20) Be continually aware of and maintain the highest standards of personal hygiene and dress.

(21) Attend meetings and training courses as required.

(22) Demonstrate awareness of hotel policies and procedures and ensure all procedures are conducted safely and within the guidelines.

(23) Be aware of duty of care and adhere to occupational, health and safety legislation, policies and procedures.

(24) Be familiar with property safety, first aid and fire and emergency procedures and operate equipment safely and sensibly.

(25) Initiate actions to correct a hazardous situation and notify supervisors of potential dangers.

(26) Strive for constant improvement and take responsibility for your own performance.

(27) Adhere to Hotel Handbook and general policies and procedures.

(28) Build and maintain positive relationships with all internal customers and guests in order to anticipate their needs.

(29) Create a positive hotel image in every interaction with internal and external customers.

(30) Adhere to hotel brand standards.

(31) Assist guests and escort them to locations within the hotel at their request.

(32) Demonstrate co-operation and trust with colleagues, supervisors, teams and across departments.

(33) Interact with department and hotel staff in a professional and positive manner to foster good rapport, promote team spirit and ensure two way communication effective.

(34) Be open to new ideas and make changes in the job and routine as required.

(35) Develop/update skills and knowledge (internally and externally) to reflect changed technology or changed work requirements.

(36) Seek feedback on areas of shortfall.

(37) Maximize opportunities for self-development.

(38) Ensure that your work quality meets the standards required and complete tasks in a timely and thorough manner with minimum supervision.

(39) Follow standards, policies and procedures.

(40) Be specific and clear while handing over the shift to others.

(41) Follow opening and closing procedures thoroughly.

(42) Maintain guest log book and staff log book at all times.

4. Butler (Junior)

In some hotels butlers are under Food and Beverage management but in some others they are under Front office management. No matter which department they work under they must always cooperate with Housekeeping, Front Office and Food and Beverage to fulfill their responsibilities. Their responsibilities will include, but not limited to the following.

(1) Ensure all arrival/expected arrival rooms/suits are checked and in order.

(2) Greet and escort guests to their rooms.

(3) Make sure that pantry and reception desk in your area are clean and well stocked and prepared at all times according to hotel standards.

(4) Ensure that all the requirements and needs are met and demonstrate a high and consistent level of service at all times.

(5) Ensure that all procedures and responsibilities relating to the Greeting/Arrival procedures are adhered to hotel standard procedures.

Appendix 3
Duties of Different Positions in the Hotel 酒店的工作岗位及其职责

(6) Provide quality and personalized services to guests.

(7) Build a thorough rapport with all in-house guests and maintain interactions in order to facilitate guest recognition and obtain specific individual needs, likes, and dislikes in order to maintain guest history files.

(8) Report for duty punctually in accordance to the issued department duty roster.

(9) Provide a full cashier and currency exchange service for guests.

(10) Upsell rooms/suites and cross sell all outlets within the hotel.

(11) Assist and coordinate the arrivals and departures of guests.

(12) Maintain a high level of communication and feedback within the department.

(13) Maintain the privacy and ensure the security of in-house guests.

(14) Handle guests' luggage and other baggage.

(15) Ensure cleanliness of suites for guests.

(16) Manage guests' special requests delivery.

(17) Identify and anticipate of guest needs and immediate action on all of their request and requirement.

(18) Ensure that all room/suites are maintained and serviced as required.

(19) Provide exceptional and memorable services to guests throughout their stay.

(20) Manage guests' garment pressing, shoeshine and other services.

(21) Follow-up and ensure that guests' requests are met in a timely manner.

(22) Complete guests' orders as per the hotel standard.

(23) Coordinate laundry, pressing collection and delivery.

(24) Liaise with other department such as finance, housekeeping, food and beverage etc. in order to achieve the guests' expectation.

(25) Attend daily shift briefings.

(26) Taking order for private dining (in some hotel which means Room Service).

(27) Deliver and place the evening amenities or gift.

(28) Unpack/Pack guests' luggage as requested.

(29) Provide a full shoeshine service.

(30) Provide tea, coffee and beverage service to all rooms/suites.

(31) Deliver newspaper and magazine to all rooms/suites.

(32) Report any suite maintenance requirement according to standard procedures.

(33) Assist and co-ordinate all in room/suite guest needs and requirements.

(34) Refresh the rooms/suites and assist with turn downs.

(35) Ensure a full and complete shift handover.

(36) Maintain full control of private bar replenishment, control and ordering of stock.

(37) Continually check all public areas inside and around the designated work area.

(38) Co-ordinate and liaise at all times with the Butler Order Taker/Butler Team Leader.

(39) Perform other duties and responsibilities as required.

(40) Abide by all policies and procedures as laid in the Butler Services SOP Manual.

(41) Adhere at all times to the butler's grooming and uniform standards.

(42) Abide by all hotel and company policies and procedures.

(43) Adhere to all hotel health and safety policies.

5. Commis

The commis chef assists the head chefs in preparing food while building his culinary skills and experience. Commis chefs often cycle through various positions during their tenure in order to help them learn different techniques, meaning that their duties and responsibilities vary. Their responsibilities will include, but not limited to the following.

(1) Produce food of high quality according to standard recipes.

(2) Ensure required mise en place is complete prior to your outlets opening hours.

(3) Ensure all orders are prepared to the correct standard.

(4) Ensure the kitchen is kept clean and tidy and take part in the cleaning schedule.

(5) Check the fridge daily for expired items.

(6) Receive delivery items and make sure they are flesh and as per requested.

(7) Take inventory off the kitchen and order required items.

(8) Carry out any additional tasks and all other duties assigned during the day.

(9) Assist with the preparation, presentation, decoration and storage of the following dishes: meat dishes/meat marinades/carve meats/fish and shell fish/sauces for fish and shell fish/garnishing techniques and methods of service for fish/buffet food (preparation and storage).

(10) Communicate politely and display courtesy to guests and internal customers.

(11) Provide direction to the kitchen helpers, including cooks, kitchen attendants and stewards.

(12) Communicate to your superior in any difficulties, guest or internal customer comment and other relevant tasks.

(13) Establish and maintain effective employee working relationships.

(14) Attend and participate in daily briefings and other meetings as scheduled.

(15) Attend and participate in training sessions as scheduled.

(16) Prepare in advance food, beverage, material and equipment needed for the service.

(17) Clean and re-set your working area.

(18) Implement the hotel and department regulations, policies and procedures including but not limited to: House Rules and Regulation/Health and Safety/Grooming/Quality/Hygiene and Cleanliness.

(19) Perform related duties and special projects as assigned.

(20) Demonstrate awareness of all the policies and procedures and ensure all procedures are conducted safely and within the guidelines.

(21) Be aware of duty of care and adhere to occupational, health and safety legislation, policies and procedures.

(22) Be familiar with property safety, first aid and fire and emergency procedures and operate equipment safely and sensibly.

(23) Initiate action to correct a hazardous situation and notify supervisors of potential dangers.

(24) Log in security incidents and accidents in accordance with hotel requirements.

(25) Coordinate and cooperate with fellow employees and seniors at all times.

(26) Ensure the smooth running of the outlet.

6. Room Attendant

Sometimes referred to as chambermaids or housekeepers, room attendants are responsible for the cleanliness of rooms in hotels, motels and resorts. Their responsibilities will include, but not limited to the following.

(1) Demonstrate and promote a strong commitment to providing the best possible experience for guests and employees.

(2) Clean assigned guest units in accordance with company standards.

(3) Stock and maintain housekeeping cars and storage rooms.

(4) Report maintenance issues to Rooms Inspector/Manager immediately.

(5) Properly tag lost and found items and turn them in to management.

(6) Perform towel service responsibilities as needed.

(7) Offer guest assistance when needed whenever possible.

(8) Comply with all safety and security policies in accordance with company standards.

(9) Report daily to the Housekeeping Office in complete uniform, pick up clean rags, section slips and sign at the key control log book for keys to the floors.

(10) Make sure that room attendant's trolley is properly supplied and clean and orderly maintained.

(11) Bring trolley to the designated floor only after through checking.

(12) Clean floor corridors, service areas, backstairs, linen closets and room attendants/maids' comfort rooms.

(13) Serve all occupied VIP rooms and guest rooms assigned to him/her according to standard procedures.

(14) Handle guest requests like providing extra beddings or offering a certain kind of food (serving food is in some hotel only).

(15) Clean all checked-out rooms in order of priority specified by Floor Supervisor.

(16) Perform maintenance cleaning in vacant rooms.

(17) Report to Housekeeping Office or Floor Supervisor immediately on any emergencies such as over-flowing toilets, fused light bulbs, etc. and other fixtures or items that may need repair and maintenance.

(18) Report to the Housekeeping Office or Floor Supervisor on any illness or accidents befalling guests, including any other irregularities.

(19) Implement the hotel and department regulations, policies and procedures including but not limited to: House Rules and Regulation/Health and Safety/Grooming/Quality/Hygiene and Cleanliness.

(20) Bring immediately to the Housekeeping Office and items that are left behind in check out rooms, making sure that it is properly registered in the Lost and Found log book.

(21) Report any unfinished assigned rooms to the Floor Supervisor for endorsement to the next shift.

(22) Make sure that linen closet and room attendants' / maids' comfort rooms are kept locked when not in use.

(23) Turn in all soiled rags, newspaper and floor keys to the Housekeeping Office before signing out of work.

(24) Ensure that storage area or pantry area is always maintained and well stocked.

(25) Perform other related jobs that may be assigned.

(26) Take inventory of the minibar to bill guests for anything consumed and restock anything that was taken out (in some hotel this is done by Food and Beverage Department).

(27) Ensure that all appliances and electronics, such as coffee pots, hair dryers, televisions, and heating and cooling elements, are functional.

(28) Take inventory of housekeeping items in the room, reporting anything that is missing or damaged.

(29) Adhere to Hotel Handbook and general policies and procedures.

(30) Provide information when requested and promote hotel's services, facilities and special events.

(31) Build and maintain positive relationships with all internal customers and guests in order to anticipate their needs.

(32) Anticipate guest needs, handle guest enquires, and solve problems.

(33) Provide extra customer service, such as turning down beds, delivering newspapers and picking up dry cleaning or ironing and fulfill requests for extra pillows or towels.

7. Bartender

Their responsibilities will include, but not limited to the following.

(1) Clean agreed designated areas, in accordance with the procedures, routines and hygiene requirements.

(2) Change table linen as required and ensure dirty or damaged linen is counted and exchanged for clean, usable items.

(3) Ensure that flowers and table decorations are flesh and comply with agreed standards.

(4) Set tables according to hotel standards, ensuring that all items used are clean, undamaged and in a good state of repair.

(5) Ensure sideboards on stations are adequately stocked with replacement cutlery, linen or

Appendix 3

Duties of Different Positions in the Hotel 酒店的工作岗位及其职责

other established needs, be they food or equipment.

(6) Maintain outstanding knowledge of cocktails, beverage and wines.

(7) Display excellent attention to detail and consistency.

(8) Anticipate guest needs and expectations at all times.

(9) Report any guest complaints and suggestions to the Outlet Manager on duty.

(10) Ensure that adequate stocks of beverage are requisitioned on time.

(11) Maintain the mise en place of clean equipment, condiments, tray cloths, cocktail napkins, etc. as per the standard operating procedure.

(12) Mix and serve alcoholic and nonalcoholic drinks to the customers of the bar or prepare for the restaurants staff, following standard recipes.

(13) Mix ingredients, such as liquor, soda, water, sugar, and bitters, to prepare cocktails and other drinks as per standards.

(14) Serve beverages to customers and offer snacks or food for them as per availability and procedures.

(15) Order or requisition liquors and supplies from the store.

(16) Make sure all the necessary items in the bar and properly arranged and stocked.

(17) Arranges bottles and glasses to make attractive display.

(18) Arrange, prepare and make slice and pit fruit for garnishing for drinks or cocktails.

(19) Upsell food and beverage items at all times and cross sell other departments or outlets.

(20) Take orders from customers and ensure these are given to the appropriate person.

(21) Inform customers of daily specials, bartender special, chef special, snacks of the day or any other promotion running in the hotel.

(22) Anticipate guest needs, handle guest enquires, and solve problems.

(23) Provide information when requested and promote hotel's services, facilities and special events.

(24) Be totally familiar with the composition of all menu items and how to prepare it.

(25) Serve food and beverages in accordance with the hotel standards, but above all in a professional, courteous manner.

(26) Clean tables and ensure they are cleaned as soon as it is apparent that customers have finished their food or drink with all acceptable balance between speed, yet allowing customers to finish their meal or drinks without feeling rushed.

(27) Ensure that customers are correctly charged, present the bill and take payment from the customer, in accordance with the procedures of the establishment.

(28) At all times be aware of and practice good customer relations, assisting the guest in any way which does not adversely affect other customers.

(29) Be continually aware of, and maintain, the highest standards of personal hygiene and dress.

(30) Attend meetings and training courses as required.

(31) Demonstrate awareness of hotel policies and procedures and ensure all procedures are conducted safely and within the guidelines.

(32) Be aware of duty of care and adhere to occupational, health and safety legislation, policies and procedures.

(33) Be familiar with property safety, first aid and fire and emergency procedures and operate equipment safely and sensibly.

(34) Initiate action to correct a hazardous situation and notify supervisors of potential dangers.

(35) Strive for constant improvement and take responsibility for your own performance.

(36) Build and maintain positive relationships with all internal customers and guests in order to anticipate their needs.

(37) Create a positive hotel image in every interaction with internal and external customers.

(38) Adhere to hotel brand standards.

(39) Assist guests and escort them to locations within the hotel at their requests.

(40) Demonstrate co-operation and trust with colleagues, supervisors, teams and across departments.

(41) Interact with department and hotel staff in a professional and positive manner to foster good rapport, promote team spirit and ensure two way communication effective.

(42) Be open to new ideas and make changes in the job and routine as required.

(43) Develop/update skills and knowledge (internally or externally) to reflect changed technology or changed work requirements.

(44) Seek feedback on areas of shortfall.

(45) Maximize opportunities for self-development.

(46) Ensure that your work quality meets the standards required and complete tasks in a timely and thorough manner with minimum supervision.

(47) Follow standards, policies and procedures.

(48) Work effectively with customers and colleagues from different viewpoints and cultures.

8. Demi Chef De Partie

Their responsibilities include, but not limited to the following.

(1) Ensure that all stocks are kept under optimum conditions.

(2) Ensure that all dishes are being prepared to the correct recipe and to the correct quantity.

(3) Assist head chef to plan menu and other necessary items for the kitchen.

(4) Ensure that all dishes reach the hot plate or possess correct garnished, the correct portion and size, presented on the prescribed serving dish in the prescribed manner.

(5) Ensure that his section is being kept clean and tidy at all times.

(6) Ensure that junior cooks and trainees receive the right training and optimum guidance.

Appendix 3
Duties of Different Positions in the Hotel 酒店的工作岗位及其职责

(7) Ensure that any anticipated shortages are communicated promptly to the sous chef or head chef.

(8) Ensure that no horseplay is allowed in his section and that all staff under his control are treated fairly and with courtesy.

(9) Deputize in the sous chef's absence and take charge of the kitchen when directed to do so.

(10) Attend training courses and seminars as and when required.

(11) Direct the preparation, seasoning and cooking of salads, soups, fish meats, vegetables, desserts or other foods.

(12) Help head chef on planning and pricing the menu and its items.

(13) Keep records of everything happened in the outlet.

(14) Check the quality of raw and cooked food products to ensure that standards are met.

(15) Monitor sanitation practices to ensure that employees follow standards and regulations.

(16) Check the quantity and quality of received products.

(17) Order or requisition food and other supplies needed to ensure efficient operation.

(18) Supervise and coordinate activities of cooks and workers engaged in food preparation.

(19) Inspect supplies, equipment, and work areas to ensure conformance to established standards.

(20) Determine how food should be presented, and create decorative food displays.

(21) Instruct cooks and other workers in the preparation, cooking, garnishing, and presentation of food.

(22) Estimate amounts and costs of required supplies, such as food and ingredients.

(23) Collaborate with other personnel to plan and develop recipes and menus, taking into account such factors as seasonal availability of ingredients and the likely number of customers.

(24) Implement the hotel and department regulations, policies and procedures, including but not limited to: House Rules and Regulation/Health and Safety/Grooming/Quality/Hygiene and Cleanliness.

(25) Perform related duties and special projects as assigned.

(26) Demonstrate awareness of all the policies and procedures and ensure all procedures are conducted safely and within the guidelines.

(27) Be aware of duty of care and adhere to occupational, health and safety legislation, policies and procedures.

(28) Be familiar with property safety, first aid and fire and emergency procedures and operate equipment safely and sensibly.

(29) Initiate action to correct a hazardous situation and notify supervisors of potential dangers.

(30) Log security incidents and accidents in accordance with hotel requirements.

(31) Coordinate and cooperate with fellow employees and seniors at all times.

(32) Ensure the smooth running of the outlet.

(33) Make employee roster as needed.

9. Doorman &Door Girl

Their job descriptions and responsibilities will include, but not limited to following.

(1) Make sure doors are open for every guest and they are properly greeted as per the hotel standard.

(2) Ensure that lobby area is clean, neat, and tidy.

(3) Give directions to the guest if necessary.

(4) Call porters or assist guests on their requests.

(5) Call taxis if requested.

(6) Ensure that entrance to the hotel is always clear.

(7) Fond farewell to the guest in proper manner and as per the regulation.

(8) Ensure all the maintenance report are properly requested and followed up.

(9) Maintain standard of front of the house.

(10) Adhere with hotel emergency procedures.

(11) Complete knowledge of hotel layout and facilities.

(12) Be aware of special facilities / services for disabled people.

(13) Be aware of airport shuttle times.

(14) Assist guests and escort them to locations within the hotel at their requests.

(15) Always comply with hotel procedures, rules and regulations on how to greet the customers.

(16) Follow safety policy at all times.

(17) Demonstrate awareness of hotel policies and procedures and ensure all procedures are conducted safely and within the guidelines.

(18) Be aware of duty of care and adhere to occupational, health and safety legislation, policies and procedures.

(19) Be familiar with property safety, first aid and fire and emergency procedures and operate equipment safely and sensibly.

(20) Initiate action to correct a hazardous situation and notify supervisors of potential dangers.

(21) Adhere to Hotel Handbook and general policies and procedures.

(22) Provide information when requested and promotes hotel's service, facilities and special events.

(23) Anticipate guest needs, handle guest enquires, and solve problems.

(24) Create a positive hotel image in every interaction with internal and external customers.

(25) Adhere to hotel brand standards.

(26) Assist guests and escort them to locations within the hotel at their request.

(27) Demonstrate co-operation and trust with colleagues, supervisors, teams and across departments.

(28) Interact with department and hotel staff in a professional and positive manner to foster

good rapport, promote team spirit and ensure two way communication effective.

(29) Be open to new ideas and make changes in the job and routine as required.

(30) Maximize opportunities for self-development.

(31) Ensure that your work quality meets the standards required and complete tasks in a timely and thorough manner with minimum supervision.

(32) Follow standards, policies and procedures.

(33) Control or monitor parking or provide valet service (in some hotel).

10. Guest Relation Officer

Their responsibilities will include, but not be limited to the following.

(1) Greet, receive and conduct guests to tables, ensuring that they are properly attended to.

(2) Ensure that guests receive best courtesy while arriving at the hotel.

(3) Ensure that phone calls are answered within 3 seconds and in proper phrase standardized by the hotel.

(4) Ensure that reservations are noted down properly (if necessary).

(5) Make sure entry door area is clean and tidy.

(6) Maintain the cleanliness of the hostess desk and surrounding area.

(7) Answers guests' enquiries regarding food, service, charges, shows, promotional offers, etc.

(8) Accept and follow-up on table reservations as prescribed by existing procedures.

(9) Coordinate with Captain in making necessary arrangements according to floor plan for reservations, blocking off reserved tables, etc.

(10) Greet guests, escort them to their table, pull seat out for the ladies, and present menus.

(11) Channel complaints and suggestions to personnel concerned.

(12) Keep an eye on entire guests' requests and follow up with server if necessary to make sure guests' requests are fulfilled.

(13) Assist in the maintenance of log book containing actual number of guests, covers, employees' absence or on leave, guests' comments or complaints, etc.

(14) Offer amenities to guests after their meals.

(15) Maintain the condition of menus. Sort out soiled or torn menus and secure new ones whenever necessary, before each meal service.

(16) May be assigned to perform clerical duties such as typing and filing reports, memos and forms.

(17) May assist in the preparation of periodical reports and time sheets for the outlets.

(18) Comply with the hotel rules and follow the standard procedures.

(19) Adhere to hotel brand standards.

(20) Maintain hygiene at all times.

(21) Assist guests and escort them to locations within the hotel at their request.

(22) Communicate with other departments on guest requests and needs and create guest history and file it properly for future references.

(23) Monitor work done by maintenance or other departments as per the outlet request.

(24) Make sure of available and unavailable items in kitchen and mention it in briefing.

(25) Upgrade and arrange notice board at all times.

(26) Follow up all outgoing requests and upon its completion file it properly for future references.

(27) Monitor and upgrade log book, tip book or any other outlet communication book.

(28) Perform other F&B duties assigned by the captain or manager from time to time.

11. Banquet Servers

Banquet servers work for hotels, resorts, conference centers, caterers and restaurants. They are responsible for banquet functions and conferences. If the banquet halls are unoccupied then they might have to work in other food and beverage outlets. Their descriptions and responsibilities will include, but not limited to followings.

(1) Maintain personal hygiene, approach and uniform clean, neat and tidy as per the hotel standard.

(2) Set up the banquet room as specified by the customers.

(3) Make sure while moving chairs and tables follow the standard procedures.

(4) Set tables to laid-down standards, ensuring that all items used are clean, undamaged and in a good state of repair.

(5) Set up the table according to the hotel standard.

(6) Provide excellent food and beverage service for banquet events.

(7) Be totally familiar with the composition of all menu items.

(8) Serve food and beverages in accordance to the hotel standards, but above all in a professional, courteous manner.

(9) Explain the food or beverage if necessary.

(10) Assist customers if needed.

(11) Keep the buffet area neat and selections well stocked (If buffet only).

(12) Ensure sideboards on stations are adequately stocked with replacement cutlery, linen or other established needs, be they food or equipment.

(13) Ensure that soiled plates, cutleries, glasses are cleaned properly from the table and stock in well-organized manner as per the hotel standard for the dishwashers.

(14) Ensure soiled lines are exchanged properly.

(15) Ensure banquet equipment are stored in appropriate places.

(16) Take inventory as per the hotel procedures and report to senior staff.

(17) Issue or report damage, maintenance, breakage promptly.

(18) Ensure that service standards are always maintained.

(19) Ensure food safety regulations are followed at all times.

(20) Prepare mise en place, refill side stations, and prepare table set ups.

(21) Serve beverage as per the functions requirement.

(22) Ensure beverage are served appropriately and follow hotel standard.

(23) Attend required training as per the outlet demands.

(24) Adhere hotel rules and regulations and follow standard procedures.

(25) Obtain necessary food handling and hygiene certificates.

(26) Maintain back of the house, front of the house, and side work duties for overall productivity of banquet events.

(27) Follow health and safety practices at all times.